BEHIND YOUR BACK

CONFIDENTIAL EMAILS EMPLOYEES SEND TO ME

BUT NOT TO THEIR BOSS!

by

Bill Cummings (Dr. C)

authorHOUSE™

1663 Liberty Drive, Suite 200
Bloomington, Indiana 47403
(800) 839-8640
www.AuthorHouse.com

© 2005 Bill Cummings (Dr. C). All Rights Reserved.

No part of this book may be reproduced, stored in a retrieval system, or transmitted by any means without the written permission of the author.

First published by AuthorHouse 05/23/05

ISBN: 1-4208-2150-4 (sc)

Printed in the United States of America
Bloomington, Indiana

This book is printed on acid-free paper.

THIS BOOK

IS DEDICATED TO

MY HONEY,

ANN CUMMINGS,

ONE OF AMERICA'S FINEST

ENTREPRENEURS

INTRODUCTION

Several years ago, "Dr. C." began appearing on TV every Monday and Friday morning in a show called: "Off To Work With Dr. C. ". I give advice to people as they race around their kitchens, feeding their kids, gulping their coffee, and getting prepared for another "day at the office".

Gradually, these viewers began sending me emails, describing their problems and asking my opinion. It didn't take me long to recognize that the "major problem" was the Boss.

In my Management Consulting work, I would ask the Boss if his people gave him good constructive feedback, and the answer was always: "Boy! Do they ever. My employees are not bashful". But when I asked the employees the same question, they'd laugh and say: "You've got to be kidding!"

This book is a summary of the emails I have received over the past several years, and my answers "on the air".

I hope you enjoy it, and, if you're the boss, I really hope you won't say:

That's not me
They're talking about.

Table of Contents

1. **A good Coach** 1
   Not a dictator, not a micromanager; not one who intimidates and embarrasses. But one who helps me to grow.

2. **A good Decision-Maker** 36
   Not one who has to be right all the time, nor one who never makes a decision. But one who is efficient and treats me like a partner.

3. **A good Listener** 51
   Not one who "multi-tasks" while listening, nor one who shows me no respect. But one who has learned to be "totally present".

4. **A good Communicator** 64
   Not one who exaggerates, nor one who hoards information. But one who has learned the "Reagan Style" of communication.

5. **A person of Integrity:** 81
   Not one who breaks promises, nor one with no common sense; not somebody who is phony and unfair. But someone who really "walks the talk".

6. **A person with Self-Confidence:** 98
   Not defensive, not arrogant, not mean. But someone who is accessible, and teaches me how to learn. Someone who doesn't rely on Product Knowledge to be our Leader.

7. **A person who builds lasting Relationships:** 119
   Not someone who builds competition, or fosters favoritism, or has to have it "her way". But someone with passion and understanding.

BE
A
GOOD COACH

Bill Cummings (Dr. C)

HE NEVER LEARNED TO BE A BOSS

"Dear Dr. C.,

"Give me something I can show to my boss. Something simple that he can understand. He's a great engineer, but he was never trained to be a boss.

"Isn't there something like "The Ten Commandments for Bosses"?

Signed: "Jonathan"

The news has been full of the Ten Commandments lately --the hanging of them; not the keeping of them.

But it gives me the opportunity to tell you about a different set of commandments. These are called the leadership commandments, and we have only two.

You can hang these commandments on the wall, and – like the ten commandments- they won't do you a bit of good unless you practice them.

You could be a teacher, or a parent or a supervisor or a manager – or an engineer. It doesn't matter. These two commandments, if followed religiously, will turn you into an excellent leader.

Here they are:

The first commandment is:

"Thou shalt catch them doing it reasonably right,

and praise them."

And the second commandment is like unto the first, and it is:

> "Thou shalt catch them doing it wrong,
>
> and coach them".

Catch them. This means you have to find them; you have to be with them; you have to know what they're doing.

Reasonably right. This means you can't wait for perfection. If the student got an "f" in math last week, but he gets a "c" this week – that's reasonably better.

Praise them. Many managers have a problem with this. They ask: "why praise people for just doing their job?" And the answer is: "so they'll keep doing it." We don't hesitate to praise our children when they do better; why not our employees?

The second commandment is:

Catch them doing it wrong. Many employees have told me: "That's the only time my boss talks to me". But the idea here is to catch them making a mistake –not to criticize, not to condemn, not to embarrass - but to coach.

We don't like to make mistakes, and when we do the wrong thing, we don't need our boss to punish us; we punish ourselves. What we need is coaching. Teach me how to do it correctly. Guide me. Help me. Coach me. Tell me you believe in me. Tell me I'm better than this mistake.

And then, when I do it right the next time, praise me.

These two commandments
Contain all you need to know
To lead

Bill Cummings (Dr. C)

SHE'S NOT A COACH

"Dear Dr. C.,

"My boss read "One Minute Manager", and she's really trying to follow it. She praises us and corrects us, and does this very well. But we need more that this. We need to be coached."

Signed: "Jennifer".

The job of every boss is to coach. Every supervisor, every manager, every parent, every teacher needs to coach. They know they won't get results by shouting or yelling or demanding performance. It must be done by coaching.

The problem is that most managers know only the first half of the coaching job. They've read "one minute manager", and they think that's what coaching is all about:

> "Catch them doing it right and praise them;
> catch them doing it wrong,
> and teach them how to do it right"

And there's no doubt about this. Ken Blanchard was absolutely right. If you do this, you will be coaching. But you'll be doing only one half of the job. A very important half. But still, only one half. What's the other half?

Most managers, and even really great managers like the ones at GEICO, sometimes overlook the second half of coaching, and then they wonder why their employees rate them high in everything except coaching.

Well, here's the secret. The first half of coaching involves statements: "You performed way above our expectations", or: "You pressed the wrong lever on that console; here let me show you how to pick the right one. "

But the second half of coaching involves three questions. Not statements. Three questions, and here they are:

Number one: "How's it going?" Give me an overall view of what's going on. How's it going? Give me your view, your opinion, your ideas.

The second question is: "what do you need?" What could help you do your job better? Do you have the right tools, the right information, the right machines? What do you need that you don't have, and let me see if I can get it for you.

The third question is so seldom asked that most employees will be shocked when you ask it. Their eyes will widen and their mouths will stand open. Here's the third question: "How could I do a better job for you?"

I'm your manager; I'm your coach; my job is to make it easy for you to do your job. How could I do a better job? What is it that I do, or don't do, that you feel I could change?

These three questions form the second half of coaching. These questions must be asked before the game is over. What kind of a coach stays in the locker-room for the second half of the game?

If you're a manager or a supervisor or a teacher or a parent, make sure you coach the whole game.

The first half is important,
but
it's the second half where the game is won.

Bill Cummings (Dr. C)

HE MICROMANAGES

"Dear Dr. C,

"Our boss micromanages us. He assigns work and we do it. But then he sends it backs to us -to do it all over again. He's never satisfied. He has spies who report back to him if we make a mistake. He doesn't ask us for our input before he makes a decision that affects us. He says that we're "in trouble" like children who act out in school. And he's right: we're whining all the time.

Signed: "Harold."

I asked a boss once why he treated his people like children, and he said: "they're treated like children because they act like children".

It makes you wonder where this vicious cycle began, doesn't it? Do adults begin to whine and complain and throw tantrums first, and as a result, management becomes like an angry mommy? Or is it the other way around? Is a micromanaging boss the cause of whining behavior?

Whatever, it sounds pretty vicious. One feeds off the other like a pool of piranha, and nobody is happy.

What would you do?

I'll tell you what I would do.

I would have the manager and his people write down what it is that they expect from each other, and why they expect it. And I wouldn't allow any generalities; no words like: respect and loyalty and integrity and honesty.

I would insist they list nothing but behavioral items: for example: "all criticism or correction must be done in private –and the reason: because that's the adult thing to do" or: "I need your reports on my desk every Monday morning, - and the reason -because the chairman of the board needs them every Tuesday morning".

The secret of being a responsible adult – as a boss or an employee or a parent or a teacher– is really quiet simple:

Clear Expectations
And
Even clearer reasons

Bill Cummings (Dr. C)

HE DOESN'T TRUST ME

"Dear Dr. C.,

"My boss doesn't trust me. He gives me a project, and then stays on my back every day with suggestions. He asks me to do some research, and I find out he's looking at the same sources.

"The only conclusion I can come to, is: he doesn't trust me."

Signed: *"Looking for a job".*

What a sad email! Here's an employee who wants to work. She knows she's competent and knowledgeable, and quite capable of doing the job. But her boss feels compelled to micromanage her. He sends the message loud and clear: "I don't trust you".

Why would a boss do that?

Three reasons come to mind.

One: the employee isn't trustworthy. She has proven over time that she can't get the numbers right, or she can't get the information on time, or she just doesn't know how to do the job. In this case, the manager needs to replace her – not micromanage her.

Two: the manager is a control freak. It really doesn't matter how competent the employee is – the manager has a data-monster inside of him. The data-monster has an insatiable appetite for reports and numbers and variances. And if the data monster is not fed daily, the manager dies. Control-freak managers need to kill their monsters.

Three: the manager is micromanaged. We don't think of this very often, but I'm finding that this is the cause of the problem more often than the first two reasons. It all flows down hill, doesn't it? Think about this: the president screams at his vice president for saying: "I don't know the answer to that question, but I'll find out for you".

Is it any wonder that the vice president blows up when his director says the same thing to him? And that the director turns on his manager, and the manager turns on his supervisor, and the supervisor threatens to fire his employee when none of these people have the answer immediately?

And is it any wonder that all of these people – if they want to keep their jobs – will find ways to micromanage- and not to delegate?

Delegation means:
"I don't have all the answers
Right now."

Bill Cummings (Dr. C)

IS SHE EFFECTIVE?

"Dear Dr. C.,

"We are constantly being evaluated by our bosses. Are we allowed to evaluate our bosses? How would I judge my boss's effectiveness? I don't see everything she does. But, of course, she doesn't see everything I do, either.

"I'd just like to know if she's really effective."

Signed: "Maria"

We speak about our effectiveness all the time, don't we? For example, we talk about salespeople: "does he get results?" "Does he bring in the sales?" "Does she meet her budget?" "Is she effective in closing the sale?" And in general, we know what that means, and we can answer it.

But a boss's product is all of us. We are the object or the effect of her concern and efforts. We grow the revenue; our boss grows us. How can anyone evaluate how effective our boss is – based on the criteria of "growing us?

Unfortunately, most bosses never rate themselves on how well they're growing us; they rate themselves on the bottom line that we generate. But there is one way to evaluate a boss on her true effectiveness. All we have to do is analyze the jobs of everyone who reports to her, and ask the question: do these people have:

More responsibilities than last year.

If you want to track your boss's effectiveness, just take a look at each person in her department.

A small TV station is a good example. This news department grows people like a gardener grows flowers. Producers and directors and reporters and anchors and video journalists and audio experts. Most of them come to work straight from school. After very few years, they have grown into first class professionals. Then they're ready to move on to bigger stations in larger towns.

A small TV station usually has effective managers. They're dedicated to growing this talent, even though they know they'll lose them.

Now, how about you? Do you have an effective manager?

What are you doing this year that you've grown into? What couldn't you do last year because you didn't have the knowledge or the experience – that you're doing this year? Are you growing?

Your manager's effectiveness
Is measured by
How much you grow.

Bill Cummings (Dr. C)

IS SHE INEFFECTIVE?

"Dear Dr. C.,

"You said last week on TV that the effective boss is one who measures how well we are growing in our jobs. Can I assume then that the ineffective boss is just the opposite?

"That is, if my boss is not helping me to grow, she's clearly ineffective?"

Signed: *"June".*

Well, it really is a little bit worse. The ineffective boss not only refuses to measure our growth – but she is also blind to the consequences.

I remember a hospital administrator in my company who bragged to me about the way he hired and fired the people in dietary and housekeeping. He hired them in at minimum wage, and worked them hard for a year. Then he fired them, and started all over again.

"Why are you doing this?" I exploded. "This is insane!"

"Oh no, you don't understand", he said, "think of all the money I'm saving you by not giving them raises."

Most ineffective managers think they're effective. They think they're saving the company money. They have no training bills, no seminars and educational expenses. When they hand in their budgets, they have no increases on the salary line.

They think they're heroes, and feel they should be rewarded.

But here's a well-kept secret:

> "Ineffective managers kill the company slowly"

It takes awhile. Most company cultures still reward the manager for financial results instead of people growth. And many ineffective managers will get promoted because they increase the bottom line—for a while.

I received an email last week from an owner of a business who complained to me about her people. "They're not motivated", she said. "They're out there making calls, but they're not reaching their goals".

I wrote back and said: "I'd have to know more about your business, but maybe it's not a case of motivation. Maybe it's a case of training. Maybe your employees don't know how to close a sale."

The effective manager travels with her employees, sits with them, talks to them, listens to them, and learns their weaknesses. Then she sets up training programs, on the job mentoring, outside speakers, web sites, books and videotapes.

The ineffective manager looks only at the bottom-line, and as it shrinks, she cries.

*Ineffectiveness
is a cancer;
You need to cut it out!*

Bill Cummings (Dr. C)

HE INFURIATES US

"Dear Dr. C.,

"Every supervisor or manager starts off by wanting to be a good boss. I'm sure that mine did. He didn't prepare for this job by dreaming up ways to infuriate us.

"What happens along the way to change that?"

Signed: *"Johnnie"*

I've wondered the same thing. But I've come to the conclusion that many of them don't know what a good boss really is; they don't know the definition.

Some of them think their job is to control their troops like a top sergeant controls his green recruits. Some think they have to hover over their people like a mother hen, watching their every move, and correcting every step they make.

I've had bosses who shouted orders several times a day; I've had bosses who never talked to me for weeks at a time.

What is the definition of a good boss?

To a child, the boss is either mom or dad – or both. To a student, the boss is the teacher. To the worker, the boss is whoever signs his paycheck.

What do all of these bosses have in common? What is it that mom and the teacher and the supervisor can do- to make them all good bosses?

Just one thing: a good boss is one who helps me grow.

Parents help me grow intellectually, emotionally and spiritually. I will do some dumb things, but they are always there for me. My growth can be stunted or enhanced by what my parents do and say.

Teachers help me grow by helping me to think. A good teacher is a good boss if she challenges me to stretch my limited horizons; to think out of the box. I won't get all "A's, but that won't matter if I've really learned how to think.

Managers help me grow by giving me the chance to make mistakes. Like parents and teachers, managers have to realize that I can only grow in this organization, if I try it. I will never grow into a mechanic by reading a book; I will never grow into a pilot by watching planes fly overhead. I will never grow at all if my manager keeps saying: "You're too new at this" or "Wait till you've been here as long as I have".

Parents and teachers and managers – all have the same basic problem: they want to leave the bird in the nest. But "birds got to fly". Otherwise, they're not birds.

If you feel you're ready to do that work, to take that project, to handle that job – tell your boss today. And if your boss says: "You're not ready yet" –ask the question: "What do I have to do to be ready?"

Don't let your life
Be
A
Catch 22

Bill Cummings (Dr. C)

SHE NEVER CHECKS BACK

Dear Dr. C,

"I've got a namby-pamby boss. She's pretty good at delegating work to be done, but she never checks up to see if or how it got done. Projects go on for months and even years. I can't depend on anybody in this place. And I can't work this way. How can I tell her?

Signed: "Hubert".

Well, Hubert is right. Every boss has an obligation to the whole company to follow up. It's just like a mother who tells her son to clean up his room. If she never checks his room, she can't congratulate him for doing it right, or correct him for doing it wrong. It doesn't take a kid very long to realize it's not that important.

And it doesn't take a worker very long either.

Some bosses, however, hate to appear authoritarian. Checking up makes them feel like spies. If your boss feels like this, ask her to establish these three things every time she delegates anything to anybody. Set:

1. The deliverable.

2. The date.

3. The reward.

Set the deliverable. Every project or task has something very concrete that will be delivered when it's finished. It's usually a report, but it could be a sale. Both the boss and the employee need to agree what this deliverable will look like.

Secondly: Set the date. This is the day the employee agrees to finish the project, and bring it to the boss. The boss is not going after it; it's the job of the employee to bring it to her.

And thirdly: Set the reward. Most bosses think that if they can't give money, they don't give anything. This is so wrong. Bosses can give plaques and little statues and certificates and a free lunch. Things that cost little or nothing at all. The president of Electromech in Wrightsville bet his vice president a dollar he couldn't get a report to him in a week. You know he got it.

What's due?
When's it due?
What's the reward?

Bill Cummings (Dr. C)

I HATE PERFORMANCE APPRAISALS

"Dear Dr. C.,

"My boss has scheduled my yearly performance appraisal for next week. I really hate this. For a whole week, I won't eat right. I'll have an upset stomach, constant headaches, and I'll snap at my children. And after it's over, and my boss has rated me on a scale of 1-5, I'll get such a small raise it won't be worth the pain.

"Why do we do this, Dr. C?"

Signed: "Don't use my name on the air".

I have worked with hundreds of companies around the world, and it is my opinion that the majority of performance appraisal systems are evil. Workers are intimidated, insulted, defeated and deflated. What good is that? Why would any organization deliberately design a system that de-motivates the employees?

If I were going to design a performance appraisal system, I'd start by abolishing it. I'd announce to everyone: "we no longer have that evil system – it's gone forever. Here is what we have instead: it's called mentoring".

Here's how mentoring works:

> Everybody in the organization has a mentor. In most cases, this will be your boss – but not necessarily. Your mentor will meet with you for at least an hour, every month. You will share with your mentor two basic things:

1. Your performance goals.

2. Your behavioral goals.

All year long, you and your mentor will discuss ways for you to reach and exceed both of your goals, and you will keep the score. And when it comes to your raise at the end of the year, there will be no surprises since both of your goals will be measured objectively and numerically.

The mentoring system eliminates two basic evils:

1. The boss who plays God. No boss can judge your energy, initiative, and drive, as well as your inner orientation to results- unless, of course, your boss is God.

2. The rating system. To rate an employee's performance on a scale of 1-5 leaves the employee bitter and bruised, crushed and dejected, and certainly, feeling inferior. Nobody gets straight "5's". It is, in the words of Dr. Deming: "a deadly disease."

To move from appraising to mentoring is like moving from darkness to light.

My advice:
Flip the switch!

Bill Cummings (Dr. C)

THE COACHING BOSS

Dear Dr. C:

"I work for a fantastic company. We don't have performance evaluations or performance appraisals any more. Our bosses refuse to evaluate us the way they evaluate a set of numbers. Our system boils down to a monthly meeting that focuses on:

1. Successes

2. Improvements

3. Coaching

"It's so simple. I tell my boss where I've been successful during this past month, and where I think I've really made some progress. And she congratulates me. Then I mention places where I've screwed up, and she helps me to understand why. And she'll add mistakes if I forgot them or didn't know I did them. Finally, she spends a few minutes coaching me on things I can do this coming month. It takes about 20 minutes, and I love it."

Signed "Jason"

Jason is so fortunate. His company really understands employee motivation. The old evaluation system never worked because it de-motivated people. It rated people on a scale of 1-5. If I'm not a "5", I'm de-motivated.

Jason's system is so much better. It allows bosses to be coaches, not policemen. It allows employees to be active not passive. It takes away all the guesswork and all the subjectivity. It replaces all that garbage with sound performance criteria. And best of all: it's monthly, not yearly. It's right now when you need it, not at the end of the year when it's too late.

Dr. W. Edwards Deming was my mentor and my friend. He lived to be 93 years old, and he never grew tired of challenging top executives.

These executives had lived with the "Performance Appraisal" system for as long as they could remember, and Dr. Deming condemned it. He called it: one of the 7 Deadly Diseases.

Sometimes they said he was gruff and even a "curmudgeon", but they always welcomed him back.

Judges evaluate prisoners.

Coaches guide winning teams.

Bill Cummings (Dr. C)

SHE INTIMIDATES ME

"Dear Dr. C.,

"I love my boss. She's the best thing that ever happened to me. I've learned more from her than all of my five previous managers put together.

"However, every once in a while she does things that intimidate me. She doesn't even know she's doing it. She sends me a stinging email, or she lashes out at me in a meeting, or she says my idea is stupid. She doesn't know how much this hurts.

"What can I do, Dr. C.?"

Signed: "Rhonda".

Well, Rhonda is not alone. She is now a member of this huge group of people in organizations all over America, who have intimidating bosses. These are technically competent bosses, some of them truly smart who —except for this one flaw – are really bosses you'll love. They teach you the business; they promote you; they pay you good salaries, and they give you great raises.

But they have one weakness. They have tongues like knives. They cut you up one side and down the other and leave you bleeding in embarrassment, while they walk away whistling.

And Ronda's right; they don't know they're intimidating. They don't have the faintest idea that they have made you feel worthless; they don't realize the pain they have inflicted. Now, we have all seen and worked for mean and ugly people; but these are not mean people. These are great people. If they truly knew what kind of frustration and shame and chaos they inflicted, they would never do this again.

If we have this kind of boss, we already know what we have to do; we have to confront him. And this is probably the most difficult thing we've ever done.

Here are 3 things to remember when you tell him:

1. Don't be a crybaby. Wait until you can talk to him without a lot of emotion. You want to be able to quote his statements or read his emails in a factual, business-like voice.

2. Accept responsibility. Make sure he understands that you know what your job is, and when you screw up, you expect him to correct and guide you, but not with intimidating overtones.

3. Don't tell him what he needs to do. Just present the data, and let him make his own decisions. If you have given him enough examples, he will clearly see the kind of behavior he exhibits that causes intimidation.

What have we got to lose? If he doesn't understand, or if he understands but refuses to change, it can't be any worse than it is now. But just think how great it can be if he actually changes! Remember:

1. No emotion
2. Accept Responsibility
3. Back off.

Bill Cummings (Dr. C)

HE EMBARRASSES ME

"Dear Dr. C.,

"I'm not afraid of my boss on a day to day basis, but I am afraid to bring him bad news. If my sales numbers are down, if my customer-satisfaction rating is low, if my work just isn't up to par, I avoid him. I know he'll find out anyway, and he'll embarrass me in our next staff meeting, so I'll try to be sick that day.

"This just isn't right, is it?"

Signed: "Martha".

No, it isn't right. It isn't right for Martha, and it isn't right for Martha's boss, either.

It's not right for Martha because she is not perfect. Like you, Martha is an imperfect human being working in an imperfect environment for an imperfect boss who represents an imperfect company. If you're afraid to go to your boss with your imperfect numbers, it means you think he's perfect, and you're not.

Your boss should welcome your problems. That's the purpose of his job. When you can't figure out why your sales dropped, or even if you can, your boss is there to coach and encourage you, not to scare and frighten you. He is just as imperfect as you are.

No, fear is just not right for you.

And it's not right for your boss, either. In fact, "scary bosses" do not *want* you to be afraid to come to them. Really. I know this for a fact. The problem is that your boss doesn't realize the impact of his position. He doesn't realize that his words and actions can pump out fear simply because he's the boss.

Last week a very powerful boss in Atlanta tore into his employees, criticizing them in public for their low performance. Later, he told me: "that should get them moving". He thought his tirade was motivational. He actually thought that his people would react in a positive way to his negative, fear-producing speech. And he sincerely wonders why his people don't ask him questions.

The president of Medtronic, Art Collins, is heading up one of America's most admired companies. He put it this way in the latest Fortune magazine; "you've got to give people the opportunity to make mistakes", he said, "and not crucify them for doing so."

70% of American workers
- like Martha-
feel they're being crucified.

Bill Cummings (Dr. C)

WHO'S THE IDEAL BOSS?

"Dear Dr. C.,

"You talk so much about "bad bosses". If you could design the ideal boss, what would this boss look like? Regardless of the gender, what would this person be doing on a day-to-day basis?"

Signed: *"Richard."*

Well, what role is a boss supposed to play? In reality, what good are they? Do we really need a boss? Could we get along just fine without one? Think for a moment about what you would do at work today if your boss resigned. I don't think things would change that much, do you? You would continue to perform your job; you would turn out the same amount of work. For a while, anyway.

So what good are bosses?

I think there are three things bosses are really designed to do:

Number one: <u>set the goal.</u> Each boss in each department and in each company should set out the goal for this year, and perhaps for this month. And this goal must be communicated clearly to everyone.

Number two: <u>reward the people</u> who are meeting and exceeding the goal, and coach those who are trying, but not quite making it.

Number three: <u>get rid of all the garbage</u> that gets in the way, and keeps the workers from working.

That's it. That's all there is. Three simple functions. That's what the ideal boss does. Most of the time, we don't even hear or see this boss. We come to work each day like a runner in a marathon. We don't have to worry about the track; it's clear of all debris. We don't have to worry about the drinking water; it's there on the tables as we run by. We don't have to worry about the goal line; it's all lit up with plenty of people around to cheer.

And that's the way our work should be. Our job is to run and win the race. Our boss's job is to clear the path, get out of the way, and let us run.

And when we've hit our targets and crossed the finish line, we hardly know who arranged the race and cleared the track and gave us what we needed to run. When we step up to get the winning medal around our neck, our bonus and our raise, the ideal boss is clapping and cheering in the background.

The ideal boss is:

1. A Visionary
2. A Cheerleader
3. A Garbage man.

Bill Cummings (Dr. C)

WHERE CAN I FIND A GOOD ONE?

"Dear Dr.C.,

"I have had so many bosses during my career, it would be hard to count them all. Some were good; some were bad, at least, from my perspective. But not everyone would agree with my assessment.

"Is there some objective measure, Dr. C., that we could apply to all bosses?"

Signed: *"Jeff"*

Well, let's think about our boss. This is the person who sets our long-term goals. This is the person who evaluates our work. This is the man or woman who determines the amount of our raise, if, indeed, we get one.

But most of all, this is the person whose main job is to help us do our jobs. Everything else that our boss does is secondary. His primary job is to focus on our needs, our concerns, our problems, our ideas, and our dreams.

The role of our boss is to insure that we have everything we need to do our jobs. Do we have the right tools, the right information? Do we have the proper lighting, the proper computers? Do we have the pay plan that is both market-driven and adjusted by our productivity?

Our boss is not there to make us happy. We are the only ones who can make ourselves happy. But our boss is there to try to eliminate all those things that make us unhappy and unproductive.

Does this sound like your boss? Does this describe the daily activities of the person you call boss?

I can hear three answers to this question:

Number one: yes, that's my boss. I have the kind of boss who talks to me several times a day, who praises and congratulates me when I do it right, and teaches me when I do it wrong. My boss listens to my concerns and my ideas.

Number two: well, I don't know if that's my boss or not. I have no idea what's going on in his head. I don't talk to my boss that much; I work very independently. I'd be delighted if I found out that he was thinking of me, and watching out for me, and trying every day to make my job easier. But I just don't know.

Number three: I know. That's not my boss. My boss is concerned about one person. And that person is not me. The only time I hear from my boss is when I've screwed up. My boss is too busy to listen to anything I have to say. My boss is offended when I mention mistakes that we've made. If his primary job is to help me, he's got a problem with his priorities.

Which of the three is yours?

1. My Reality?
2. My Dream?
3. My Nightmare?

Bill Cummings (Dr. C)

WE GET WHAT'S LEFT OVER.

"Dear Dr. C.,

"I work in a small Georgia town, and I guess I can't expect to have a boss who's a great leader. Atlanta has great leaders, and Washington, D.C. But our little towns get what's left over.

"Why does it have to be this way?"

Signed, "Henry."

Nothing could be further from the truth. When it comes to leadership, the size of the community makes no difference at all. The skills in the leader whom Donald Trump hires in New York City will be the same skills that are found in Wrightsville, Ga.

The president of Trump Real Estate must have the same skills as the president of Electro-Mech Scoreboard Company in Wrightsville. Both leaders will be asked to do exactly the same thing.

Every leader – regardless of the size of their community – can communicate by voice mail, email, telephone, fax, and in person. We all have the same tools.

The difference is not in the size of the city, but in the quality of the leader. I have seen poor leaders in San Francisco, and excellent leaders in Wrightsville, Ga. Likewise, I worked with a fantastic leader in Rome, Italy, and with an egomaniac in a small city here in Georgia.

The size of the community means nothing; it's the size of the leader that counts. How do we size up a leader? How do we take the measure of a good leader?

Here are six questions you can use if you're a leader:

1. Do you know how to listen? Politicians on the campaign trail are asking questions in every town they visit, but seldom do they listen to the answers.

2. Do you know when to stop listening and when to start doing something? Once you have all the data you can get, you have to act.

3. Do you know how to" wow your customers"? The successful companies in the world today are filled with leaders who write every job description with the customer in mind.

4. Do you know how to build lasting relationships? Real leaders are in this game for the long-term results, not for short-term band aides.

5. Do you know how to coach? The best leaders are not bosses, they're coaches. They don't shout and scream at their people; they guide and teach and mold their people.

6. Do you know how to give away the credit? The great Japanese philosopher, Lau Tsu, said of the truly great leader: "when his team has succeeded, they barely know he exists".

Any leader
In any city
Can do these six things

Bill Cummings (Dr. C)

HE JUST CAN'T COACH

"Dear Dr.C.,

"There's just no hope. My boss doesn't get it! He feels the only way to get productivity is to beat on us.

"People are leaving here in droves, and the clown still refuses to face reality. He praises no one; he's never around; he can't possibly know what we're doing. And yet, if his Division is to succeed and if he is to get a Bonus (or even just keep his job) – we're the ones who must do it.

"It's like he's never heard of "coaching"!

Signed: *"Pete"*

My grandson Michael is 10 and he plays for the Athletics in a league with regular pitching. Austin is 6 and he plays for the Bluejays with a pitching machine. My wife and I sit in the bleachers with the other parents and grandparents and we shout and scream and laugh and cry as this great drama plays out in 5 or 6 innings.

But as I sit there watching, I keep wishing that every manager and every owner and every corporate executive- every boss - could see this. I wish they could inject the same kind of enthusiasm in their workers that these coaches inject in these little kids.

I taught the executives at Georgia Tech for 4 years while Bobby Ross was the head football coach. Bobby and I agreed on these 3 principles that every coach and every boss should use:

1. Teach the basics every day

2. Let the players play the game

3. Play to win.

Teach the basics. You don't see this watching the Braves on TV, but you see it all the time in little league. Between innings, the coaches are constantly showing the kids how to hold the bat, and how to catch the ball. How many bosses are providing us with the kind of training we need? All of us can improve. Do we have a coach who really cares to help us?

Let the players play the game. Even when their team is loosing, the coach can't bat for them. The coach can't run out to shortstop, and catch the grounder. The players play the game. The coach watches. But how many bosses micromanage? How many bosses can't stand to let us make a mistake? How many bosses don't know how to coach?

Play to win. Every coach plays to win. No matter how far behind the team might be, the coach keeps telling his players they can win. Every boss should be like that. Every worker should know what it takes to win, and how to learn from a loss. When the ballgame is over, these tiny kids gather around the coach. If they won, they celebrate; if they lost, they're told they can win the next time.

Every coach is a leader.
But not every boss is a coach.

Bill Cummings (Dr. C)

WHY DO WE NEED A COACH?

"Dear Dr. C.,

"My Boss asked me the other day: Why do we need a Coach? We're all grown up; we've got families and jobs and responsibilities. We're not in school any more. Why should we look around for somebody to coach us? Wouldn't that indicate a lack of self-confidence? Wouldn't that seem like a weakness?

"He means it. What do I say?"

Signed: *"Henry".*

Well, I think that's precisely what it is. All of us are weak – from time to time. There's not one person reading this who doesn't put emotion before logic every once in a while. And when that happens, we need a coach. We need someone who listens to us, and someone to whom we listen.

A vice president called me last week. I have been working with her for the past 6 months, helping her to make a very delicate and complicated decision with her life. But last week, she almost undid all the work we've done. She felt her president had insulted her. She was furious, and she was ready to quit. If she hadn't talked to me, she probably would have quit, and it would have been a terrible mistake.

Whom do you call when you're having one of those days? Who is your coach?

It should be someone who can put everything else aside, and can give you a prompt and in-depth opportunity to talk. A chance to vent; a chance to explain, and then a chance to explore all the possibilities.

Do you have somebody like that?

It should be someone who can keep a confidence; someone who knows the value of secrecy and confidentiality. Someone who will never reveal your confession.

Is your coach like this?

It should be someone who gets to know you even better than you know yourself. Someone who can penetrate your facades, who can know the "real you".

Can your coach fill these shoes?

When I was in the monastery, we called this person "our Father Confessor". We went to him every week, and he coached us with great wisdom and sensitivity. When I joined the business world, I found a few managers who possessed this remarkable skill, and they used it almost daily as they "managed by walking around". When I got married, of course, my wife assumed this role, and still does it better than any priest or president.

All of us need a coach.

Who fills that role
For you?

Bill Cummings (Dr. C)

BE
A
GOOD DECISION-MAKER

SHE'S GOT TO BE RIGHT

Dear Dr. C.,

"My boss is really great – as long as I agree with her. She's a good listener and a good delegater and a good communicator. But the minute I say something she disagrees with, she gets defensive and blows up.

"It's just not worth it any more. So I never tell her how I feel about certain decisions. And I think that's sad.

Signed: "Gina"

One of the best listeners I ever met was my college Scripture professor. Not only did he treat us with respect and dignity; not only was he always present when we spoke to him, but he had a third quality that was truly unique.

He encouraged all of us to disagree with him. He welcomed wild and different ideas. He didn't reject us out of hand the way most professors did when we said stupid things. I remember one day he listened intently as I told him I thought St. Paul was gay. "Really!" He said. "Show me why you think so".

Everything we said was important to him; every idea we had, meant something to him. Even when we knew he disagreed 100% with our theory, he not only listened, he encouraged us to explore it and expand it.

I have met very few bosses who do that.

Does your boss do that? Does your boss take the time to listen to you even when you know he disagrees with you? That's a special talent, isn't it? Would you like to learn how to do it?

It's not easy, but here's the secret: it's called: "what if". Children do this instinctively. Last Christmas, we gave my 5 year old grandson, Austin, a Spiderman outfit. We helped him put on the suit, and the mask and the webbed hands and feet, and he walked around the living room enjoying all the applause.

Then, when no one was watching him any more, I saw him walk into the next room alone. He put his webbed hands on the wall and then one of his webbed feet, and then he tried to walk up that wall.

Sure, even at 5 years old, Austin knew he couldn't walk up the wall. But, now with his Spiderman outfit on - what if – what if he could?

That's the secret. No matter what someone says to you; no matter how "off the wall" the statement is, what if, what if it could work?

That's how the greatest listeners do it.

They're not patronizing you; they're not playing games with you; they are sincerely asking: "What if?"

They're putting aside all their own experience and knowledge, and they are giving you a chance to prove your point; to make your case, and in the process, to even prove them wrong.

Try this today. Instead of saying: "you're wrong!" when you know deep down he is, sit back, and think: "what if he were right", and then say:

"Talk to me about that".

You never know.

*Your very own Spiderman
may climb your wall.*

HE WON'T GIVE ME A RAISE!

"Dear Dr. C.,

"What's the secret for getting a raise? I've been here now for 18 months, and my boss has never once mentioned the possibility of a raise.

"How do I go about negotiating what I want?"

Signed: *"Jenny"*

Do you ever try to get someone to do something they don't want to do? Of course, you do; just about every day! You try to get your kids to eat the right kind of food; you try to get your husband to wear the right kind of clothes; and of course, you try to get your boss to give you the right kind of raise.

It's called negotiation. But how can we negotiate if I keep saying "yes" and you keep saying "no"?

Well, there are two techniques I have learned over the years that might help you. The first one I call "jujitsu". I can't guarantee it will get you the raise you want, but it might help you with your kids.

You know how jujitsu works. If I start to hit you, your immediate reaction is to block my fist with your arm. But jujitsu teaches us just the opposite: "grab my arm and pull it towards you, and you can flip me right over your head."

Jujitsu negotiation is doing just the opposite of what comes naturally. When you shout at me – instead of shouting back, which is what I feel like doing – I listen patiently while you continue to shout. When you tell me how wrong I am, - instead of me telling you how stupid you are, I ask you to explain.

It's simply amazing how quickly this will defuse an angry scene. Even with your kids.

Once both of us are calm and collected, we can begin to look at the problem, and why each one of us wants a different outcome. And this is the second technique I try to use. You must ask "why" do I want this, and "why" do you want that?

Schoolteachers face this every day. "Michael, I want you to read this book on the American Revolution". And Michael says: "I don't want to read that book".

Ask "why"? Why does the teacher want him to read? And why does Michael not want to read? The teacher wants Michael to learn the story of the revolution, and she knows that she learned that story by reading. But Michael has dyslexia, and he doesn't learn by reading. He learns by hearing.

So the problem is not: "reading or not reading". The problem is "learning or not learning." And you can only find that out by asking why.

If the teacher had said: "Here, Michael – watch this public television program on the American revolution, Michael would get straight "As.

When you sit down with your boss to talk about your raise, you might want to remember:

Play jujitsu
And
Keep asking: why?

THEY'RE REALLY INEFFICIENT

"Dear Dr. C.,

"I get so frustrated at work. There are so many thing I could do if they would just back off. They treat me like a child. I am perfectly capable of ordering supplies, delegating projects, and arranging my own schedules. But no! I have to ask permission like a 3rd grader. It's so inefficient"

Signed: *"Marvin."*

I feel for Marvin. Last weekend, I went fishing with my 7-year-old grandson, Austin. He's about 3 feet high, and doesn't weigh more than 50 lbs, but he wants to do everything his big brother does. He snagged a branch in the bottom of the pond and was frustrated because he wasn't strong enough to pull it up by himself. He kept saying: "I can do it; I can do it".

But he couldn't. He just wasn't strong enough. This is understandable; what's happening to Marvin isn't.

Little Austin is held back because of his size and strength; Marvin is held back because of his position in the company. Austin will grow out of his dilemma; Marvin won't.

I remember the look on a corporate secretary's face when I asked her for a pencil. She hung her head, and said: "not only do I not have any extra pencils, but I'm not allowed to order them".

The one that is hilarious- if it weren't so ridiculous- is the grocery store clerk who cannot cash your check. She holds up the whole line behind you while she shouts into the loudspeaker: "manager to the check-out". Everybody waits while the manager comes up from the back of the store. He looks at your check, takes out his pen, writes his initials, and hands it to the clerk.

How efficient is that?

Employees are told to "think out of the box". But sometimes their box is so small they're liable to smother. How can I be creative, how can I take risks – if I have to ask permission for everything I do?

I have a suggestion:

1. Make a list:

Write down all the decisions- or even just one- that you feel you could make, but are not allowed to make because of some rule or regulation.

2. Show it to your boss:

Make sure it's the right time for him. Some like the mornings; other prefer the afternoons. Make sure he's got the time and the inclination to listen.

3. If he says "no", ask why not.

Ask it respectfully, but let him know you're really interested in the reasons. Sometimes when bosses begin to explain the reasons, the opposite becomes crystal clear.

Healthy children grow
up
Healthy employees grow
Out

SPLIT DECISIONS

"Dear Dr. C.,

"Do you ever hesitate to make certain decisions at work? I know what my job title is; I know what my job description says – but how about this decision, right now? Do I make it, or does my boss make it? Let me give you an example. I'm a teacher; two of my students start fighting in the back of the classroom."

"Are there any guidelines, Dr.C.?"

Signed: *"Harriet."*

We all know that job descriptions and job titles don't help us with job decisions. And it's a job decision that will make or break the day.

Here's a little technique that really helps. Think of all the decisions you faced during the last month, and put them in three levels:

    Level one: do it; don't tell the boss.

    Level two: do it; tell the boss later.

    Level three: don't do it; till I talk with the boss.

<u>The level one decisions</u> are ones you make every day just to get your job done. If you're a teacher, you're deciding which learning tools to use with dyslexics and which learning tools to use with readers. You don't have to tell your boss about these decisions.

<u>Level two decisions</u> are still within your scope of authority, but because you know your boss is going to hear about them, you want to be the first to tell him. If you punish those two boys who are fighting in the back of your classroom, and one of them is the headmaster's son, you'll want to tell him before his son gets home.

Level three is a decision you are asked to make, but it's simply outside the level of your authority. If you get a call from a parent, asking you to skip her child into the next grade, you can't make that decision alone.

Now here's the key: after you have written down all the decisions that you can remember, and you have put them into these three levels, set up an appointment with your boss, and ask these two questions:

1. Are these decisions in the right levels? If not, let's change them now. If I'm bothering you with a level 3 decision when you really want me to make the decision and tell you later – I'll move it into level 2.

2. When I make level 2 decisions, do you back me up even if you disagree with what I did? After all, this is the only way I can learn and grow.

It should not be a
Tough decision
To make a
Tough decision.

I FEEL LIKE A SLAVE

"Dear Dr. C.,

"I know bosses are busy. But so are we. Why can't my boss treat me like a partner? Why can't he take the time to ask me – before dumping a new project on my desk? Sometimes, I feel like a slave!"

Signed: "Janice."

Janice is absolutely right. We "partner" with other people, don't we? Let's say you think you want to get married. Or you think you might quit your job. Or you're thinking about investing some money in the stock market. You wouldn't dare do any of these things without talking to someone you trust.

All of us have partners. People we trust.

Well, how about work? How about the decisions our managers make every day at work? How about the assignment of that report to Jane or that complicated job that ended up on Ron's desk, or the project the boss asked you to complete by the end of the week?

Bosses make these decisions every day, don't they? Many of them – like Janice's – never ask. They have no idea what else we're working on, or what we'll need to put on hold if we take on this new project.

Some managers say they don't have time to ask. They barely have time to delegate. If they consulted with their people before they delegated the work, nothing would get done.

Besides, consultation sounds like a partnership. In many companies, the relationship between the manager and the people is not a partnership; it's a benevolent dictatorship. Much like Mommy and the child, or teacher and the student, or kind master and the slave.

But what if we became partners? What if managers thought about their people as partners? Instead of telling people what to do, and giving them orders and assigning them projects, what if the manager asked: "How do you think you could get this done?

Instead of saying to us: "I want this on my desk yesterday", what if he asked: "When can you finish it?"

Instead of that famous phrase that all of us have heard: "get it done or else", what if we heard: "What else do you have on your plate for today?"

If I am treated like a child, I will act like a child; if I am treated like a slave, I will act like a slave.

*Partners get things
Done.*

THEY DON'T ASK!

"Dear Dr. C.

"I'm an orderly in a health care facility. That's about as low as you get on the food chain. I'm not important like the R.N.'s and the Administration. I give back rubs and empty bedpans and I transport patients in wheelchairs.

A month ago, Administration made the decision to buy our wheelchairs from a different company. They didn't ask me. When the new ones came, they had a faulty breaking system. I complained, but nobody listened. One of our patients was severely injured last week. Why don't managers ask?"

Signed, *"Charles."*

Well, managers are just like the rest of us, I guess. Sometimes, they just don't think. But Charles' example is being repeated all over America, this very morning.

Supervisors are ordering materials; managers are writing procedures; directors are dictating policy, and all of this: without asking the people who know. City and county officials are making decisions about our community; state representatives are voting on important issues, without asking those of us who will be affected.

Why does this happen?

The answer, however, is no further away than our own home. What kind of family decisions do we make without asking our children? Don't we get in the habit of saying: "I know what's best for my child"?

Managers feel this way, too. I'm sure the purchasing director said: "I know a good wheelchair from a bad one; I don't have to ask an orderly."

Now, managers can't go around asking people before they make *every* decision; that would be impractical and impossible. But I hear Charles saying: "when in doubt, ask". It only takes a moment, and it could save a lot of pain and money and embarrassment.

I remember driving up to the curb side check-in area at the Atlanta Airport. The cars and busses were 3-deep. Everybody was honking and shouting and one policeman was running up and down trying to keep order.

I stood in the crowded street, holding my bags and looking to see where I could find a place to check-in. The tall, black check-in Agent caught my eye, and waved me over. When he finished checking me in and handed me the boarding pass, I waved my hand over the chaotic scene in front of us, and said: "I bet you could design a user-friendly check-in system".

He smiled sadly and said:

Generals
Don't Ask
Privates.

HE CAN'T MAKE DECISIONS UNDER PRESSURE

"Dear Dr. C.,

My boss finds it difficult enough to make regular decisions, but making them under pressure is beyond him. I know there are no two pressure-filled decisions that are identical, but isn't this type of thing a regular science; something that could be learned?

Isn't there some system he could learn?

Signed: "Jeff"

Well, Jeff is right: no two pressure-filled decisions are identical. For example, take the Clinton decision to attack Bosnia and the Bush decision to attack Iraq. Both were preemptive strikes and in both cases the U.S. became the aggressor. But the pressure of 9/11, and the closeness of Syria and Iran to the Iraqi borders changes the present danger considerably.

However, regardless of the pressure, there's a science involved. In each case all six scientific steps had to be followed, and here they are:

1. Define the problem

2. Measure the seriousness

3. Find the root cause

4. Brainstorm solutions

5. Pick one and act.

6. Measure the results.

These are the scientific steps each warring president must follow, and they are the same steps you and I must follow whenever we have to make a serious decision under pressure.

For example: let's just say that you're unhappy at work.

#1. Define the problem. This may take a long time, but stick with it. Is the problem your boss, your fellow workers, your work itself, or maybe you? If you don't define the problem, you'll end up solving the wrong thing.

#2. Measure the seriousness. On a scale of 1-10, where would you put it?

#3. Find the root cause. If you decided that the problem is the lack of communication between you and your boss, dig deep to find the root cause. It's down there, believe me.

#4. Brainstorm solutions. Once you have the root cause nailed down, realize that there are many solutions. You could take him out to dinner or you could simply talk to him in his office.

#5. Pick one and act. It may be the wrong one. That's okay. You can always try another solution. Keep going till it works.

#6. Measure the results. Now on a scale of 1-10, where would you put it?

*Follow these six steps,
and you'll have great success
in making decisions under pressure.*

Behind Your Back

BE
A
GOOD LISTENER

Bill Cummings (Dr. C)

HE DOESN'T LISTEN

"Dear Dr. C.,

"I know I'm not the most important person on my boss's radar screen, but I do have things he needs to hear. Why won't he listen? Is it me?

Signed: "Frances."

As I travel around the country, I hear this complaint more than pay and benefits, more than politics or favoritism. "Not-listening" seems to be the number one complaint.

Why do bosses shut us out? Why won't bosses listen?

Most experts in this field point to 3 primary causes.

The first one is: "background noise". If a child grows up doing her homework with a loud TV or radio blaring in the background, she will probably be the boss who listens to her voice mail while you're trying to give her your report. She calls it: "multi-tasking".

The second is status. This is so common we forget the impact it has on listening. All through school, we watched a few of our teachers who were cold as ice to us, but warm as toast to the principal. They hung on every word the principal uttered, but didn't hear a thing we said. Some bosses listen intently to their boss – but don't hear a word that comes from us.

The third is the "ghetto mentality". It's called prejudice. It's the most difficult to overcome. We can turn off the background noise; we can eliminate the status symbols; but it's almost impossible to overcome prejudice.

We are all born into some kind of ghetto. Mine was an Irish Catholic ghetto; yours might have been an African American ghetto; some grew up in the Country Club ghetto, and others in the Southern Baptist ghetto. "Ghetto-thinking" goes like this: "We're right, and you're wrong." If I don't belong to my boss's ghetto, she will have some very subtle, and many times unconscious, blocks when she tries to listen to me.

Getting your boss to listen is more complicated than it should be. But just knowing this, might help.

Bosses must overcome
Background noise, status and the ghetto mentality,
Just to hear your words.

Bill Cummings (Dr. C)

HE'S INSENSITIVE

"Dear Dr. C.,

"Maybe I'm asking for too much. Maybe my boss is just too busy, or maybe I don't understand the 'business culture'. But I know I would work a lot better if my boss were more sensitive.

"He doesn't see our problems; he doesn't feel our pain; he doesn't hear our complaints. Even when we try to explain, he just doesn't listen. He's completely insensitive.

Signed: *"Martha".*

There are two ways to listen - both at work and at home. You can listen to the words, or you can listen to the meaning behind the words.

Most of us feel we're doing well if we can just listen to the words. Life is moving at such a fast pace. At work, we're doing more - with less people, and at home, the bills come in faster than the income. When we hear people talk, or read a memo or play our voice mail, most of us are thinking: "hurry up, hurry up - get to the point".

We barely have time to listen to the words; how could we ever take the time to listen to the meaning behind the words?

But this is the kind of listening every boss must learn. Whether we're the supervisor or the president of the company. Whether we're the headmaster or the teacher in the school. Whether we're the parent or the grandparent – we must learn to listen to the meaning behind the words.

It's like a song. If you erase the music, the lyrics sound hollow. Even rap songs, which have little melody at all, make better sense with the beat - than just reading the words on a page.

How many times have you criticized your boss's memos – only to find out later that's not what he meant at all? How many times have you been crushed when someone read what you had written, and confronted you in anger? How many times have you punished your child – and found out later that you understood him incorrectly?

How can we get behind the words? How can we cure ourselves of this "fastest gun in the west" reaction to the words we hear?

I know of only one way: there's a very old phrase, often used in jokes about psychologists, and it goes like this: "what I hear you saying is…" And then you state very clearly what you think you're hearing. Do this with the people who report to you; do this with your boss, do this with your children.

More times than not, you'll receive an answer like this; "no, that's not exactly what I meant; I mean this." Then you say it again: "okay, now let me see if I understand; what I'm hearing is this."

People who truly listen find creative ways to pose the questions, but when the message – or the messenger- is important, they always check at least twice.

Listen to the music.
The lyrics don't tell the whole story.

Bill Cummings (Dr. C)

HE'S MILES AWAY

"Dear Dr. C.,

"You won't believe this. Yesterday, I'm in my boss's office giving him a report. He had moved away from his computer, so I thought he was really listening to me.

"Wrong!

"While he's nodding his head to me, he reaches over and hits the voice mail button on his phone!

"He calls it multi-tasking. I call it bad manners!"

Signed: Janice.

Have you ever found yourself talking to your boss, and he's not there anymore? Oh, he's present – physically. He's still sitting in his chair, but mentally, he's miles away.

That happens sometimes when I'm talking to my little grandson, Austin. I have to lean down and shout: "earth to Austin".

One of the secrets of listening is being totally present. And what a joy it is when your boss has learned this secret. The minute you walk into her office, she pulls away from her desk and her phone and her computer and all the important papers in front of her. She sits down in front of you, and listens as if you were the only person in her world.

Is your boss like this?

Or is your boss the hyperactive juggler who keeps 15 balls in the air at all times? When you walk into his office, he's on the phone but waves you in anyway. He puts his hand on the phone, and says to you:

"Yes?"

You say: "we've got an angry customer who wants to talk to you".

"Tell me about it", he whispers, and continues to talk to the person on the phone and to you at the same time.

This man is "present" to no one.

When you are totally present to another person, it's like being in a narrow tunnel. It runs from your head to his head. There's nothing on either side; no sounds can penetrate; no voices; no interruptions.

My son is 41 years old now but when he was 7, he was a "rapid fire question machine". He asked more questions in one hour than all the modern game shows put together.

But I remember one evening when I had put in a rather long day and I was sitting in my chair at home reading the paper. My seven-year-old son was sitting on the rug playing. He began to ask me questions as usual, and, as usual, I answered them in my half-conscious way while I continued to read my paper.

But this time, he suddenly stopped talking and walked outside. I had not been present to him at all. To this day, it haunts me to wonder what question he had asked that I never answered.

If you can't be totally present,
Don't be present at all.
Reschedule.

Bill Cummings (Dr. C)

HE SHOWS NO RESPECT

"Dear Dr.C.,

"Just Listening- is not enough. My boss listens to us. He sits behind his desk like the principal in my son's grade school, taking in everything we say. He nods and throws out an occasional "Hmm" and "I see" and "I understand".

"But when we finish, he dismisses our ideas as foolish and impractical and not worth pursuing. He shows us no respect whatsoever. Listening is not enough."

Signed: "Arthur."

I had a boss once who called us into his huge paneled office for a meeting, and while we were making our presentations, he was clipping his fingernails. We took bets to see if he'd remove his shoes and socks and start on his toenails.

He didn't respect us, and I can tell you for sure – we did not respect him.

Have you ever seen a boss destroy a person's dignity during a meeting? A banker friend of mine, who is now the president of his own bank, told me this story. When he was fresh out of college, he joined a bank in Arizona. He will never forget his first staff meeting with that Arizona bank president. One of the vice presidents had just given her presentation. In the presence of all the officers, this president humiliated that woman until she broke down and cried.

After the meeting was over, the president told my friend: "Well, I guess I got her attention". My friend told his new boss: "If you ever do that to me, we'll say goodbye that very day".

When a boss disagrees with what is being said, he can still treat the speaker with respect and dignity. There are two rules that every boss should burn into memory.

Rule number one: never criticize in public. Ask questions, explore the topic, pose alternatives, and yes, disagree - but don't destroy a person's dignity. If a criticism is merited, do it in private.

Rule number two: give the speaker your power. That's what listening means. You turn over your power to the person who is speaking. You give that person the same respect you expect when you're speaking.

Listening without respect
Is like
Flying without wings.
You hit the ground quickly.

Bill Cummings (Dr. C)

THEY LIKE LAZY PEOPLE

"Dear Dr. C.,

"Help me with this. Every day at work, I see people I just can't stand. They have no enthusiasm, no drive, and no personality. They never speak up, they never volunteer; they punch in every morning and punch out every night like robots. I call them drones.

"Now here's the mystery. Why do some managers really like these drones? Some of our executives here at work actually find these drones interesting and enjoyable. I don't get it. What am I missing?"

Signed: *"Janet".*

Janet is not alone. Most people simply do not understand the four different temperaments that make up our personalities. They think everybody should be just like them.

Janet has an outgoing personality, and she thinks those introverted, quiet, little drones are lazy. She doesn't realize that the drones think Janet is loud, arrogant and boorish.

Janet calls this a "mystery", and I guess it is. But it's a mystery you can unravel if you wish.

How would you like to know why the people at your job, your church or your club act the way they do? How would you like to know how they see you?

Think of the people at work who drive you crazy. Have you ever stopped to think that these same people might have strengths and talents and skills that you would die to have?

Think of Janet and her drones. Her drones listen. Janet doesn't. Her drones have patience; Janet doesn't. The drones can spend hours analyzing numbers that would put Janet to sleep.

What if Janet began to understand and appreciate the valuable aspects of her drones instead of pouncing on their weak spots?

What if you could see a one-page summary of your strengths and weaknesses? Would that help you to realize that everybody at work is different, but that they all add value?

Send me an email at doctorc@leadershipclinic.com, and I will send you a personality test you can take on line. It's a great way to start.

We cannot all be the same,
But,
We can all add value.

Bill Cummings (Dr. C)

LISTEN UP

"Dear Dr. C.,

No matter how hard she tries, my boss just can't seem to listen to us. I guess she thinks she knows what we're about to say. Or maybe she just disagrees with the first words out of our mouths. Or maybe she just has too much to do – to listen. Whatever. She's making many un-necessary mistakes."

Signed: "Linda"

"Listening intently" is called level 1 listening. Very few of you are doing that in the morning while you watch TV. Some of you are putting on make-up; or feeding the kids; or reading the paper with a cup of coffee. Very few of you are sitting down in front of your TV, watching and listening intently.

And that's okay. You're listening on level 2 or what we usually call: multi-tasking. You can easily catch the weather and make breakfast at the same time.

But the question you need to ask is: "can I catch Julie's report at work today, and view my email at the same time? Can I listen to Jim's question while I'm listening to my voice mail?

Can I multi-task, and run the chance of missing the point?

Listening intently takes 5 strategies. Here they are:

<u>Number one: ask clarifying questions</u>. People seldom say exactly what they mean. Ask them to explain it one more time. Even if you think you know what they mean, they will be happy to say it again in another way.

<u>Number two: encourage them.</u> Don't appear irritated and eager for them to stop talking (even if you are). Focus on their face

and give them your full attention. Many introverted people pick up your body language very quickly, and they'll stop talking – just when they shouldn't.

<u>Number three: paraphrase their words:</u> "what I hear you saying is …" They'll tell you if you're getting it wrong. Sometimes, just hearing you state it incorrectly helps them to state it correctly.

<u>Number four: empathize.</u> Show them you understand their feelings. Say: "you're feeling upset or betrayed", or whatever it is. You don't have to agree with their conclusions or their emotions. You certainly don't need to sympathize – but you do need to empathize.

<u>Number five: summarize their entire content.</u> "Do you think we could sum it up by saying…"

If you're doing all five, you're listening on level one.

*That's what
Real Leaders do.*

Bill Cummings (Dr. C)

BE
A
GOOD COMMUNICATOR

HE DOESN'T COMMUNICATE

"Dear Dr. C.,

"My boss can't communicate worth a damn. He moans and groans while I'm trying to explain something to him; then he cuts me off while I'm still talking; then he sends me away before he understands what I've been saying.

"I'm so exhausted –I've just given up."

Signed: *"Frank".*

It's not easy to be the "Great Communicator". I don't think it came naturally to President Reagan. It's something you learn and keep learning and keep practicing all the time.

With the President, it wasn't the words he used or even his precise diction. It wasn't even the content of his speeches. It was the way he responded to ideas and suggestions. We called it: "active response".

This is what he did:

- He smiled
- He nodded
- He repeated

I talked to president Reagan only once in the White House, and I will never forget that experience. But many of you saw him on TV when he gave his press conferences.

When a reporter spoke to him, he smiled. It was a warm, inviting smile. A smile that said: "I'm interested in what you're saying". You've seen people who frown the minute you open your mouth. The great communicator smiled. It wasn't a phony smile for the cameras; it was a "hello smile" to start communication.

Even when it was a hostile reporter, even when the topic was Olie North, he smiled. If you were going to take the time to talk to him, he greeted you with a smile.

The second thing he did was nod in agreement. It wasn't that he was agreeing with every opinion we had; he was just letting us know he understood what we were saying. It's such simple thing, but without it, communication often breaks down. I'm sure you've talked to people who sat like stones- or worse yet, looked at files on their desk, or fiddled with their pencil. The great communicator nodded as we talked.

Psychiatrists and Counselors do that. Good listeners do that. Great communicators do it all the time.

And the third thing he did was to repeat our idea. He repeated the gist of what we were trying to say. He said it in our words, and then he said it in his words. And then he'd ask us if we thought he understood.

Sometimes, we'd say: "no, that's not what we meant", and he'd start all over again until we were convinced he understood clearly what we were saying.

Only then – did he give us his answer.

If you want to be a great communicator:

Smile
Nod
Repeat

And you can be our next President

HE EXAGGERATES

"Dear Dr. C.,

"I thought Nelson Mandela was a friend of ours, His words about America this year were certainly not friendly.

"He said Americans don't care about people?! Give me a break! If we hadn't cared about him, he'd still be in jail".

Signed *"Disgusted"*.

We live in a free country with a free press. If you want to express your opinion, you're free to do so. We don't live in a communist Russia or Cuba, or in a dictatorship like Libya or in Iraq when Saddam was in charge. In those countries, you could be shot for disagreeing with your leaders.

Here in America, we're comfortable with Republicans and Democrats, with liberals and conservatives, with Catholics and Jews, and Muslims and Baptists. And that spills over to our work place, too. We feel free to criticize our bosses, our policies and even our traditions.

But sometimes, in our enthusiasm, we exaggerate. Nelson Mandela exaggerated last Friday in his tirade against President Bush. He called our President arrogant and shortsighted and implied that he was a racist for ignoring the United Nations in his zeal to attack Iraq. That was bad enough. But then he went on to say:

"If there is a country that has committed unspeakable atrocities in the world, it is the United States of America. They don't care for human beings,"

"Americans don't care for human beings"?

I winced when I read those words. And I'm sure you did, too. And then I got angry.

We don't care for the 911 victims; we don't care for the homeless and sick? We don't care for the millions of people all over the world that receives billions of dollars in aid every year? We don't have more volunteers than any other nation in the world? We don't care about the 8 astronauts who died? We didn't care about your freedom of speech, Nelson Mandela, when we printed your hate-filled words about us?

And then I stopped. I realized that he was only exaggerating. And I asked myself this question:

"Do I exaggerate at work? If I'm the sales manager, have I ever told one of my people that no one has ever sold less? If I'm the supervisor, have I ever said to one of my people: "you just don't care about the company".

Exaggeration is wonderful
In fairy tales.
But it can be lies and liability at work and in politics.

HE DOESN'T SHARE INFORMATION

Dear Dr. C.,

"I don't mind it when my boss keeps the financials locked up, but he won't even tell us how we're doing verses the competition. He attends a meeting each week with the president, and never mentions a word of what was spoken there. He criticizes my work from time to time, but has never talked to me about my career. And then he says: "be open with me". Yeah! Like I'm ever going to do that!"

Signed: "Mike".

Mike, I know what you mean. Knowledge is power, and some bosses want all of it. They're afraid to share this information with you, because they don't want to share the power that goes with it. I think every boss needs to call a meeting with his people every 6 months. He needs to ask them 3 simple questions about this information:

 1. *What do you want?*
 2. *How do you want it?*
 3. *When do you want it?*

What kind of information is necessary? That depends on the job I have. If I'm in sales, I've got to have numbers; if I'm in production, I've got to speak with vendors; if I'm in administration, I've got to see the financials. But no matter where I am, I have to know where I stand with my boss. "No information" is simply unacceptable.

How should it be delivered? Again, some of it must be: "one-on-one", because it's confidential. But most of it can be emailed. Every boss should be writing updates to his people every week. No boss should ever worry that the competition might see this. Why not let the employees see it and use it. The executives can be trusted to keep the secret; why not the employees?

And thirdly: When should it be given? The sooner, the better. Many bosses hesitate to give out the company news, until the whole town has read about it in the paper. Give it all: the bad news and the good news. The employees are grown-up folk now, and need to be treated like it. Don't put it off.

"Tell me.
Tell me all of it
Tell me now!"

I'VE ALWAYS DONE IT THIS WAY

"Dear Dr. C.,

"I've got a crew of workers who show up each day, and wait for my orders. I give the orders; they walk away grumbling and complaining, but eventually they get the work done.
"I don't like this system, but I don't know any other way; this is the way it's always been.
"Any ideas?"

Signed: "Ralph".

I wrote back to Ralph and asked him if he ever goes bass fishing. I find bass fishing very similar to a boss giving orders.

There are two basic ingredients:

1. Encourage the fight
2. Make the release

When you fish for bass, you have to keep changing your bait. Sometimes, they bite on a spinner; sometimes on a plastic worm; sometimes they want live bait.

It's probably the same thing with workers. They don't want to hear the same words in the same way every morning. Sometimes you might show a film, sometimes work off a flip chart; sometimes you might even have one of them give the orders for the day.

The second ingredient for good bass fishing is the fight. Bass love to fight. They jump up out of the water; they dive down and twist around; they do everything they can to spit out the hook. This is what makes bass fishing so much fun. It's no fun to catch a catfish; he doesn't fight.

If you're a boss like Ralph, you need to give your orders in such a way that your workers can "fight back". Most bosses present their orders like generals in a battle zone where "yes, sir" is the only response. Instead, challenge your people and give them outlandish goals and then allow them to shout back. Encourage them to come up with different ideas and different ways to hit the targets that must be reached. Encourage the fight.

The third ingredient, of course, is to make the release. After the fight, the bass fisherman removes the hook, and releases the bass to swim on his own.

Every good boss must practice the release. Let your workers swim. If you gave them the right bait, and you allowed them the good fight, they will swim for you.

*I guess workers
are a lot like
bass.*

A BOSS TALKS BACK

"Dear Dr. C.,

"I'm a boss. I watch your show every Monday and Friday, and I agree with most of what you say: many of us bosses don't listen; we don't accept feedback; we don't delegate; we don't hold good meetings; we play favorites, and we don't seem to respect our employees.

"But we're only human. Give us a break!"

Signed: *"John".*

John is right. We all deserve a break. Even the boss. But the best break a boss can get is knowledge. The knowledge of how to be a boss.

Whenever I speak to the top executives of any organization, I find myself thinking of parents. Mom and dad. When we were kids, especially teenagers, how often did we say: "she doesn't listen; she doesn't understand; or: dad is unreasonable"?

And how often do our kids say that about us?

Parents and bosses face exactly the same problem. Simply put, it is this: "how can I get other people (kids or employees) to do what I want them to do, and like it"?

Mom wants Michael to clean his room. But if mom yells at him and punishes him, Michael will never clean his room the way mom wants. It will be a never-ending fight. Mom must figure out what Michael values; is it money? Is it recognition? Is it competition with his brother? One thing's for sure: it's not punishment.

Bosses need to do the same thing. They need to study us the way mom needs to study Michael. They need to find out what we value.

However, both bosses and parents are so busy about other things; they forget their most important job.

Both scream: "give me a break". But the break they need is right in front of them. Each child is different and each employee is different. But each one of them values something. Find out what that something is, and your lives as parents and bosses will be a whole lot easier.

Bill Cosby's famous line is worth repeating here:

No matter how calmly you try to referee,
parenting will eventually produce bizarre behavior,
and I'm not talking about the kids.
Their behavior is always normal.

HE MAKES ME A LOSER

"Dear Dr. C.,

Life is not a bowl of cherries the way you seem to make it every Monday and Friday morning. At least, not in my life: my annual review was a joke, my raise was 2%, my boss avoids me, and my work is boring. I feel like a loser."

Signed: "Drew."

Drew is absolutely right about one thing. Life is not a bowl of cherries. But he's absolutely wrong that I look at life that way. I don't see our lives as something pleasant that is put before us, all washed and ready to eat like a bowl of cherries. I see our working lives as a game of golf.

The Master's tournament finished in Augusta. 93 of the best golfers in the world tried to qualify to play in this tournament. Only 44 made it. Among the 49 who didn't even get a chance to play were names like: Mike Weir and Ben Crenshaw and Jack Nicklaus and of course, Arnold Palmer. And of the 44 who actually played, only one of them won the green jacket. Does that mean that the other 92 men are losers?

Not in the game of golf.

You see, each one can look at his own scorecard and say: "I played better than I did yesterday". In the game of golf, each player keeps his own score. Each player is concerned about improving his own game. He may lose the tournament, but he can beat his game.

We can do the same thing at work. We may not get that promotion, or that 10% increase, or that bonus this year, but if each one of us keeps score, we will be winners, and not losers.

How many strokes does it take for you to get your "working golfball" into your cup at work? For some of us, it will be customer satisfaction scores, for others, it will be piecework. But each one of us knows – even better than our boss – how we can make our work a little better. Measure it each day, and keep score.

*Only people who keep score
can ever hope to win
the green jacket.*

SHE'S THE PROBLEM

"Dear Dr. C.,

I handle problems every day at work: customer problems, technical problems, employee problems. This is the reason I have a job. And I'm very good at it, too. In fact, many days I feel I handle my job-problems better than anyone else.

Except one. My biggest "job-problem" is my boss", and I just don't know how to deal with her. How about some hints.

Signed: *"Don."*

I know what Don means. Suddenly, all of our problem-solving skills seem to vanish. Everything we learned about communication and negotiation melt in our mouths like butter. We can't focus; we can't speak up; we can't think with logic because we're so full of emotion.

Now some of you reading this will laugh. You don't have this problem; your boss is delightful not frightful. You can skip this page. But for those of you who feel deeply about this, and you know who you are, what can you do about it?

Here are four steps to consider if your biggest problem at work is your boss:

<u>*Step One. Write down the facts*</u>:

Keep a journal at work. If your boss is ignoring you or overloading you or holding you up for public ridicule – whatever the problem might be - write it down. Put the date and the place and the exact words that were used. If you see that months go by without any repetition of this behavior, close your journal, go back to work, and get over it. But, if it continues, go to step two:

Step Two: Practice:

Find somebody who will help you practice the right approach. My wife is an expert in this; maybe your spouse is, too.

Step Three: Find the right time:

There are certain moments in every day when your boss is relaxed and open to listen. But if you don't have access to those moments, don't take a chance. Make an appointment.

Step Four: Speak and listen.

Lay out your case without emotion. Without anger. Without tears. Present the facts as you wrote them in your journal, and end up your presentation with this statement: "I am sure this is not your intention, but it is my perception. What can the two of us do about it?"

And then: listen. Listen and take notes.

If Silence is golden
Calm Confrontation
is Platinum

I DIDN'T GET THE MEMO

"Dear Dr. C.,

"I don't really know what just happened to me. Our company has all the latest communication systems. I have a cell phone, Internet, voice mail, a beeper, and a weekly staff meeting. And yet: My boss decides to give one of my major accounts to another salesman, without telling me? Not a word. Not a hint. I find out through the grapevine.

"By not telling me, I think he's telling me something."

Signed: "John Scared".

Well, he certainly is telling John something, and John needs to ask him right away. But I think he'll find it's always one of three things. When we "don't get the memo", it's either:

1. They forgot

2. They're chicken

3. They don't love us any more.

Bosses do forget. They're human beings just like us. They're putting out fires, talking to customers, working on the budget. Sometimes, they forget things that are very important to us. I hope that this is what happened to John, because the next two reasons are not as nice.

The second reason is that some bosses are chicken. That is, they don't want to confront us on difficult issues, so they don't involve us at all. Confrontation is always difficult, but that's a big part of a boss's job. That's one of the reasons we pay bosses more money. If your boss is simply avoiding you because he knows you disagree with him, it's up to you to confront him.

But now the third reason any one of us "does not get the memo" is because our bosses don't love us anymore. They don't think we're important enough to the organization. They don't need our input; they don't need our ideas; they don't need us.

I don't respect a boss who stoops to this level; I don't value any boss who can't take the time and effort to sit down with me and say, "I'm sorry, but this just isn't working out any more. Let me help you find another job."

I had to fire over 40 people in my career, and I didn't enjoy it at all. It was the very worst part of my job. But I never hid behind the "Whoops! Didn't you get the memo?" and hoped the person figured it out.

Every boss needs to
Communicate
The bad stuff as well as the good stuff.

BE
A
PERSON OF INTEGRITY

Bill Cummings (Dr. C)

SHE DOESN'T KNOW THE MEANING OF INTEGRITY

"Dear Dr.C.,

"My boss has no integrity at all. She gossips. She reveals secrets. She never keeps a confidence.

"It's just too difficult to work here. I can't trust her.

Signed: "Alice"

Last week I was in Oklahoma talking to a group of managers about integrity. One of the best definitions of integrity we found was this: "trustworthiness and incorruptibility to a degree that one is incapable of being false".

It's what GEICO calls: "uncompromising integrity".

Dr. Laura Slessinger says: "people with integrity do what they say they're going to do; others give excuses".

My brother joined the army in 1952 and they put him in military intelligence, taught him perfect German, and sent him to spy on the East Germans and Russians. After four years of undercover work in East Berlin, he was captured and about to be executed when he escaped, and returned home.

I asked him how he could possibly put himself in such continuous danger for 4 long years. He answered very simply: "I gave my word".

I think this is what integrity means. "I gave my word". It's not legal; it's not a binding document; it's not conditioned on how much money I make. It's very simple. "I gave my word".

I know a manager who is excellent in every way but one: he comes late to every meeting. He says he'll be on time; he even promises to make it, but he's always late. Last week was the first time he realized that people who come late – lack integrity. He'll be on time from now on.

Uncompromising integrity takes place alone and in the dark when nobody's looking; when nobody knows; when it's so easy to do the wrong thing. I over-charge a customer, but she will never know it. I drive too fast and get away with it; I do sloppy work but I cover it up. I make a promise, and hope the person forgets it.

When I worked in New York, I used to take the 20-minute helicopter ride every morning from the airport to Manhattan. One morning, Bobby Kennedy boarded and sat next to me. Both of us opened our briefcases on our laps to do a little work, when we noticed that both of us had pictures of our children on the inside flap. Now I know that the attorney general of the United States had much more important things to do that morning, but he took the time to talk about "kids" all the way to Manhattan.

Many years later, I saw this quote that Bobby had made shortly before he was assassinated. He said: "it is from numberless diverse acts of courage and belief that human history is shaped." I know for a fact that one of his beliefs was the importance of his family.

*It takes courage
To live a life of integrity.*

Bill Cummings (Dr. C)

SHE BREAKS HER PROMISE

"Dear Dr. C.,

"My boss can't keep her promises. I don't know if she just gets over-ruled by Corporate, or whether she just makes too many promises that she shouldn't.

"Whatever, we have a real morale problem here in the office because she promised everybody a 6 month raise. And we're in the 7th month already.

"Good people are going to quit if she can't learn to keep her promises."

Signed: *"Alice."*

For some people, breaking a promise is like the end of the world, and for others, it's no big deal. Which is it? Should a boss be criticized for this, or should his people just grow up. Like, welcome to the real world!

No, it's always important. Regardless of what some people may tell you, when you break your promise, it's always a big deal. You lose part of your integrity; you lose some of your trustworthiness. You become a little less than you were.

It doesn't matter what it is. You promise your boss you'll have that report by Tuesday; or you promise your son you'll take him fishing next Sunday, or you promise your spouse you'll quit smoking today.

Whatever you promise – it's your word. It's your integrity. It's literally: you.

There are three things we can do to help us keep our promises:

1. Don't make one

2. Make a commitment

3. Make a plan

Try not to promise at all. Especially to your children. Say things like: "that's a great idea, and we will see if it's possible" or: "I can't promise you that, but I will try".

However, sometimes we have to promise. Our boss says: "when can you have that report on my desk?" If we say: "I'll have it there tomorrow morning at 9:00", we have just made a promise. The minute you hear yourself making a promise to your boss, to your spouse, to your children, to your friends – to anyone; recognize that there are two more things you need to make:

1. Make a commitment. Decide immediately that nothing will prevent you from keeping this promise. Imagine every obstacle, and picture yourself overcoming each one. Play it over and over in your mind like a movie, until keeping this promise is the only possible ending.

2. Make a plan. Make it as detailed as you can. Write it down; don't trust your memory. Write down: "who what, when, where and how?" "This is what I will do, at this particular time, in my living room, using our home movies."

Don't make a promise if you can avoid it, but if you make one, plan to keep it.

Your integrity depends on this.

Bill Cummings (Dr. C)

HE HAS NO COMMON SENSE

"Dear Dr. C.,

"I have worked for doctors, lawyers, scientists and teachers. Some of them were truly brilliant people. But many of them had no common sense.

"How does this happen?"

Signed: please don't use my name on the air.

All of us have seen this, haven't we? We know that some of the most brilliant people in the world had no common sense. Remember Mozart and Einstein? And I'm sure you've seen many smart people in your own lifetime that can't control their temper, who can't listen or communicate, or have no flexibility. They can speed-read and do calculus in their heads, but when it comes to common sense decisions, they're lost.

How does this happen? I think I know.

It starts in grade school. That's where the basic test is formulated. It measures how well you will do academically. If you can read and do math, you can get a high score. You can be sure you will be promoted from grade to grade, pass your SAT with flying colors, go on to college, and get a good paying job.

But the problem is this: these tests do not measure common sense. A straight "A" student can float through 12 years of American education and never be tested or trained in common sense.

I spent 6 years consulting to the school of education in one of our leading American universities. I saw several people flunk out because they couldn't pass the academic tests, but I never saw a failing grade given to someone who didn't have the common sense necessary to teach students.

There is a "common sense" test, you know. It's called: "emotional intelligence" or EI. EI tests four basic aspects of common sense:

First: how much do I know about my emotions, especially those that come to the surface?

Second: how well do I handle those emotions, and constantly improve myself?

Third: how much do I know about the emotions of those around me, especially their politics and networks.

Fourth: how well do I help these people to improve themselves?

Emotional intelligence is common sense.
The problem is:
It's just not that common.

Bill Cummings (Dr. C)

HE WANTS TO LEARN COMMON SENSE

"Dear Dr. C.,

"I'm a medical doctor. My mother watched your program last Friday where you talked about smart people with no common sense. My mother says that's me.

"Although I may not agree with her on this, I am curious: do you really think that common sense can be learned – like medical skills?"

Signed: *"Doctor, MD".*

Most of the time, mothers know best. And this is one of those times. Yes, of course, common sense can be learned. Unfortunately, the schools don't teach it.

But common sense can be broken down into categories, just like medicine or law or science. Common sense has 4 basic skills, which require study and then practice.

The "study part" is not "book learning'"; it's observation. It's observing the way you currently handle these 4 skills, and asking others (like our mothers) to observe us also. The 4 skills are: Self-discovery, Self-Improvement, Discovery of Others, and Helping them to Improve. (The same skills as Emotional Intelligence)

The "practice part" is the tough part. It means changing the way we've been acting for the past several years. It means taking each one of the 4 skills – one at a time – and slowly making each one a part of our regular daily habits.

Let me give you an example:

The first of the 4 skills is self-discovery. Let's say you discover that you get angry at work. In fact, people have begun to avoid you because they don't want you to blow up all over them. Now, it's just common sense to do something about this, but we never learned how. Nobody ever taught us.

But if you decide to "practice" common sense, this is what you'll do: you'll realize that anger is a secondary emotion. It follows "feeling afraid, or attacked, offended, disrespected, controlled", and so on. You'll identify this primary emotion, and deal with that before you get angry. For example, you'll say to the person: "Hey, I'm feeling pressured". Most people will then back off, and you will avoid the blow up.

Now that's just common sense.

Here's a quote all doctors could frame:

"Common sense and education
are highly compatible
but
neither is worth much without the other."

Bill Cummings (Dr. C)

THEY'RE REALLY STINGY

"Dear Dr. C.,

"Each pay period when I get my paycheck, I feel bad. I look at the money that's going to the government and the percentage into savings, and what's left is hardly enough to pay my bills. Payday should be an upper instead of a downer. I don't get paid enough".

Signed: *"Lisa".*

Nobody gets paid enough. Obviously, even Bill Gates doesn't get paid enough because he's still working. So is Warren Buffet. You will never get enough on that paycheck to make you say: "Oh, that's fine; that's all I need".

So what can we do to make payday an upper? We have to start asking a different question. We have to quit asking: "How come I don't make as much as Henry?" Or "Why can't I get a raise?" These are questions that will only bring us down.

Let's start asking this question: "where did I add value during these past two weeks?" We are being paid to add value. We are not being paid to answer the phone or work on our computers or make homework assignments to a class full of children. We can get robots to do that. We are being paid to add value.

Each of us has a customer, a person who receives our work. This is someone outside our organization or someone inside. Our job is to add value to the life of that person.

When we look at our paychecks this week, let's ask ourselves: did we add value?

I'll never forget the assembly plant in Perry, Ga. that manufactured airplane doors for the Boeing 747. One man spray-painted the door, and then passed it down to another man who attached a piece of sheet metal with a grommet gun. One day the painter noticed that the sheet metal man had to spend a lot of time digging out the paint in the grommet holes before he could do his job. Immediately, the painter designed a set of plugs which he inserted before he painted the door.

Such a little thing. But he added great value to his customer. He earned his paycheck that week.

How many of us will
Really earn
Our paycheck this week?

Bill Cummings (Dr. C)

ANOTHER BOSS TALKS BACK

"Dear Dr. C.,

"Every time you talk about the "insensitive boss", I find a copy in my mail box the next day. And the day you talked about the boss who criticizes his people in public, I got 15 copies. Enough already! What am I supposed to do? If somebody said something stupid in one of your meetings, what would you do?"

Signed: *"Roger".*

Well, I suppose that would depend on what I want. If I want an atmosphere of blind obedience, I'd do exactly what Roger is doing. And 40 years ago, many successful businesses were run this way. I remember staff meetings in San Francisco in 1968 where the staff parroted exactly what the boss wanted to hear. Nobody was ever embarrassed, because nobody ever said anything "stupid".

Sometimes, however, "stupid statements" contain tiny gems of wisdom. And if we don't allow people to speak before they think, we'll never get those wild, creative thoughts that crack through our stodgy walls of tradition.

If 3m didn't allow "stupid statements", we wouldn't have the post-it note today. If Bill Gates didn't allow "stupid statements", we wouldn't have the computer world. If we don't allow "stupid statements", we won't hear that one idea that could change our whole business.

Now, I know it takes a lot of patience. And many extroverted bosses don't have time for patience. That's why many companies install an OFI system or a QI system. This allows everyone in the company to write down any idea (even a stupid one) that comes to their minds. These ideas are read and considered every week. Toyota in Japan gets thousands every day from their stores around the world. Companies find that 10% of these ideas prove to be very profitable.

But even these systems won't work if bosses make fun of suggestions that are somehow: "out of the box".

Tom Peters says, "People can smell emotional commitment from a mile away". And he's right. If my boss is committed to creativity, if he truly wants new ideas and fresh ways to solve problems, it will show. He will put up with 90% stupidity, just to get that 10% nugget of wisdom.

He will be like that little city girl who went to visit her grandmother's country farm. The grandmother found her in the manure pile on her hands and knees, pushing her way to the center. "What are you doing, girl?" Grandma said. "Looking for the pony," she replied.

*We need more bosses
who are willing to look for
the pony.*

Bill Cummings (Dr. C)

THEY'RE ALL PHONY

"Dear Dr. C.,

"You can always tell when the big shots come to town from our corporate office. Our bosses clean up their desks, wear their best clothes and their best smiles, and run scared all day.

"Why do they act so phony around authority?"

Signed: *"Joan."*

Hey! It's not just our bosses. We're guilty of that, too, aren't we? We act differently when we're meeting with our preacher or priest or rabbi. If the Pope came to town, all the Catholics would put on their best behavior. How do you act when the cop pulls you over for speeding? Why do you think our teachers say to unruly kids: "you do that again, and I'll send you to the principal"?

Authority can generate respect, or it can generate fear.

Respect is a good thing; fear is a bad thing.

Authority should be respected. When it's not, we have anarchy and chaos. We are a nation of laws. We have legislators who write our laws, and we have officers who maintain and protect our laws. These people hold positions of respect. It's the same thing at work. We have top management who sets policy and middle management who implements it. The people in these positions deserve our respect simply because of their position. It's a good thing for our company and for our country to have positions of authority when the result is respect.

But when the result is fear, it's a bad thing. When the people in these positions begin to generate fear instead of respect, they have crossed over from leadership to dictatorship. Ask the Iraqi people whether they respected Saddam Hussein, or whether they feared him.

But how can a boss here in America tell when he's crossed the line?

It's simple, really. He just needs to look in the face of the person in front of him. Respect generates questions and opinions; fear generates silence and acceptance. Respect generates creativity and independence; fear generates insecurity and dependence.

If you respect your boss, you can go to him with wild and crazy ideas, and know that he will listen. If you fear your boss, you'll say good morning, and go drink your coffee.

*Respect is exhilarating;
fear is debilitating.*

Bill Cummings (Dr. C)

HE'S NOT FAIR

"Dear Dr. C.,

"I am a single parent. I'm not complaining, but sometimes it just seems a little unfair. I do more than my share of the work, plus running off to cart my kids to games – and I get paid less than my male counterparts. Well, maybe I am complaining; I feel overworked and underpaid."

Signed: "Linda."

When I hear that phrase, "overworked and underpaid", I always think of the book of Exodus. The Hebrew people were working as slaves for the Egyptians. They were building two complete cities from the ground up, making the bricks themselves.

The Egyptians not only whipped them and beat them and paid them far less than minimum wage, but they took away the straw they needed to build the bricks. When they couldn't produce the bricks they needed, they were whipped even more.

Now that's: "Overworked and underpaid."

Lately, I'm beginning to realize that many of the women I see in companies and organizations around central Georgia can make that claim. Not all the women, but lots of them.

They start the day by making breakfast for the family, picking up the house, and driving the kids to school. Then in the middle of the staff meeting, the school nurse calls on her cell phone. Her child has a fever. Now she has to juggle picking up her sick child, and still getting this report done on time. It would help if she had a husband to lend a hand, but either she doesn't, or he can't leave his job.

Then she's back at work, racing to meet the deadline on the report. And somehow – I don't know how – she makes it.

Most men are clueless. They would never be able to do this in the first place, but even if they could do it, they would refuse to work for the pay this woman is making.

I want to pay tribute to all you women who have entered our male dominated work place. You have brought a new freshness to the stodgy dens of industry. You have brought a new level of productivity, and a new standard of behavior. There is no doubt that many of you are overworked and underpaid, but in spite of that, you make bricks without straw. You are accomplishing what many men before you could not do.

J.P. O'Rourke wrote a funny line in one of his books. Like most of his politically incorrect phrases, this will be not be acceptable to many men. It goes like this:

> *"Women are successful in business today because*
> *business was created by men.*
> *Men are babies.*
> *And...women are so good with kids.*

Bill Cummings (Dr. C)

BE
A PERSON OF
SELF-CONFIDENCE

I CAN'T FIND HIM

"Dear Dr. C.,

"I have a great boss; he knows our business; he listens intently; he's fair and honest and funny. I couldn't ask for anything more – except one thing: I never see him. He's never here. I don't know where he is.

"Is this good or bad, DR. C?"

Signed: *"Amy."*

Well, it's both good and bad. It's good because he's not breathing down your neck and micromanaging you. Some bosses can't trust us to make the sale, or write the letter, or give the speech. It's our job, but they have to do it.

Obviously, this will never be Amy's problem. Her boss is simply not there. But where is he?

A boss's job is very much like the coach of my grandson's little league baseball team. When Michael steps up to bat, the coach doesn't walk up with him. When Michael races to catch a fly ball, the coach doesn't jump up from the dugout, and run out to the field to help him.

But when Michael comes back to the dugout after hitting a home run or striking out, the coach is right there to pat him on the back. That's what good coaches do. That's what good bosses should be doing.

But where have all the bosses gone? Where is your boss? Well, I'll tell you where they are. They're not in your dugout. They're in meetings. They have at least two or three meetings a day. And when they're not in a meeting, they're answering emails: 100 a day. Or they're answering 50 voice mails or checking their beeper that vibrates constantly.

Bill Cummings (Dr. C)

Technology has caused an avalanche of information, and it all comes tumbling down like heavy snow on your boss, who is expected to shovel it, and, oh yes, be available to you at the same time.

If your boss is anything like this, email him today and say: "Hey! can I help you shovel that snow?"

Shoveling snow side-by-side
-even in silence-
is a great way to talk to your boss.

HE MAKES ME GIVE PRESENTATIONS

"Dear Dr. C.

"I love my job. I write reports; I schedule meetings; I do research, and I have a lot of confidence when I'm talking to people one on one. But the minute my boss makes me stand up in a group, I freeze. My voice squeaks, my mind goes blank, and I make a total fool of myself. Why does my boss do this, Dr. C.?"

Signed: *"Sheila".*

I know it won't help Sheila to learn that half of the men and women in business around the world have the same sweaty palm syndrome that she has. The other half of the population can't wait to stand up and talk and they don't want to sit down. We call Sheila's half: introverts, and the loud half: the extroverts.

But what can introverts do about this? I suggest three things:

      1. Breathe deeply.

      2. Make notes

      3. Talk to your boss

First: learn to breathe. I'm sure you've heard this before. But are you doing it correctly? If you stand up and breathe deeply from your chest, it won't help you relax at all. Learn to take some deep breaths from your diaphragm before you get up to talk. When you inhale, your belly should extend outwards, and when you exhale, your belly comes in. This is very important.

Secondly, always jot down a few notes if you feel you might be called on to speak. This does not indicate a lack of self-confidence; it assures your audience you will know when to quit talking.

But thirdly, if this is a severe problem for you, Sheila, and I know it is for many people, talk to your boss about it. She might be able to restructure your job, so you won't have to make these painful presentations.

*Just because you have the sweaty palm syndrome
does not mean you lack self-confidence.
But it sure makes you look like it*

SHE'S SO DEFENSIVE!

"Dear Dr. C.,

"Our boss tells us to give her "honest feedback". She prides herself on being a boss who can "take it". But the fact is – she can't. She gets so defensive and critical and angry – that nobody takes the chance.

"Maybe we don't know how to do it, or maybe she doesn't really want it. The fact is – it's not happening."

Signed: *"Anonymous"*

The question for all of us – not just our bosses – is: how do we handle honest criticism without getting our feelings hurt? And I think the answer is: we can't. Listening to critical feedback always hurts a little, no matter how it's done. The fact is: the truth hurts.

However, all of us need honest feedback for three reasons:

1. We all make mistakes.
2. We all have weaknesses.
3. None of us can grow without feedback.

Each one of us makes mistakes. We make them at home with our family. We make them at work with our team. We make them at church with the other volunteers. Sometimes people tell us, but if you're the boss in any one of these three places, chances are you won't be told.

Nearly every executive tells me: "My people give me great feedback; they never hold back". Yet when I ask the employees if they give him honest feedback, they look at me as if I had lost my mind. "You've got to be kidding".

Each one of us carries a bag full of weaknesses. Some of us talk too much; some of us don't speak up when we should. Some are too aggressive; others are too easy. We have the conservative control freaks at one end, and the liberal hippies at the other. And all of us are trying to do our best. However, common sense tells us that we are not pleasing everyone. Just as there are some personalities and temperaments that grate on us – so there are employees of yours who go home and night, sit around their dinner table with their families, and say: "Let me tell you what my dip-stick Boss said today".

But do you think for one minute they're going to tell you? Not a chance.

Honest feedback is growth food for the soul. We cannot grow into good parents, good pastors, good presidents or good bosses without it.

Young prince William of England went to an exclusive prep school these past four years after the death of his mother, Princess Diana. The only boy who ended up giving him honest feedback was a poor peasant boy who started off hating the prince.

If you make mistakes, if you have weaknesses, and if you want to grow as a human being – ask yourself: "who's giving me honest feedback?"

The answer
may surprise you.

I'M NOT ARROGANT!

"Dear Dr. C.

"I have just received some feedback from my employees. They think I'm arrogant, headstrong, and intolerant of any opinion that is not my own.

"They are dead wrong on this, Dr. C.; how can I get them to see the truth?

Signed: *"Richard."*

Well, what is the truth?

The truth according to Richard is simple. He's the boss. He's accountable for a definite number of results, and he needs to get his people to deliver those results, quickly, efficiently, with a high degree of quality and a low degree of hassle. He doesn't call this arrogance; he calls it self-confidence.

However, the truth according to his people goes like this: Richard is just like a general in charge of an army at war. He demands that his troops stand at attention, and do what they're told, and ask no questions. He's a boss who accepts no failures, and when a failure does occur, he calls the reason for the failure - an excuse. If this isn't arrogance, what is?

So what is the truth? Is Richard an arrogant, over-bearing, headstrong, disdainful, supercilious general, who shouts when he should listen? Or is he simply a self-confident, dedicated, workaholic who has fire in his belly?

What do you think? What is the truth here?

I think that every one of us who have worked for the "Richards of this world" (and most of us have) recognizes the dilemma. Drive looks an awful lot like demand; self-confidence quite often appears to be arrogance; and assertiveness looks more and more like aggressiveness. Even such a great thing as enthusiasm can be seen as intimidation.

A boss like Richard needs to do 3 things:

1. Ask for anonymous feedback.
2. Accept it
3. Change his Behavior

HE'S JUST MEAN.

"Dear Dr. C.

"I love my company and my job and my salary; I even like my boss – most of the time. However, I hate him when he embarrasses me in public. He'll cut me down in a meeting with my peer group and even in a meeting with people who report to me. He's caustic and intimidating, and just downright mean. And it's not just a male thing, either. I've got women bosses who do the same thing.

"Why do they do this, Dr. C.?"

Signed: *"Jane"*

I don't know all the reasons why bosses do this. But I know one reason why some of them do. It's part of their personality.

Bosses who are strong, driving, goal oriented individuals have this tendency. They get impatient with people who are slower and more deliberate. They want fast action. They want solutions, not problems. They want immediate results.

Do you remember the TV sit-com "Seinfeld"? The writers of that show made Elaine this type of person. She was always in a hurry. She always had "things to do". She pushed George around like he was a puppet. She had no time for his long explanations and his tendency toward perfectionism. She embarrassed him in public, in front of his friends, and felt no shame or remorse.

Many bosses – both men and women – are like Elaine. Most of them have no idea they embarrass employees, and when they find out, they say: "so what?" Public embarrassment doesn't bother them; why should it bother you? What's the big deal?

So, what can we do? If this kind of treatment really bothers you, but you don't want to leave your job because of it – I will give you two suggestions:

Number one: tell your boss.

Be very specific. Tell him exactly what he said and who was present in the room, and how that made you feel. Acknowledge that you know he doesn't mind it when his boss embarrasses him in public, but you're just different, that's all.

Number two: recognize your own weakness. If you are the quiet, dedicated employee – both loyal and trustworthy- you might be the type who's always late with your work, or who never speaks up in meetings, or who procrastinates forever.

Your tendency may upset your boss as much as his tendency upsets you. Ask him. And promise him that as he improves himself, you will improve yourself.

As my wife always says:
"What's fair's fair".

MY TURN TO BE BOSS

"Dear Dr. C.,

"I just got promoted. I'm going to be the boss, and ten people will report to me. I don't want to be a lousy leader, or even an "okay leader". If I can't be an excellent leader, I don't want this position. How can I know?"

Signed: *"Patti".*

My answer to Patti was: watch the good teachers. If you want to see leadership at its best, and you want measurements to gauge the effectiveness of good leadership – just examine the behaviors of good teachers.

Here's what they do:

First: they think about their kids constantly. They know the strengths and weaknesses of each child in their care, and their minds are continuously designing new ways to challenge hyperactive Tommy, and dyslexic Michael and quiet Austin.

How often does your boss think about each person who reports to him, and how often does he design new ways to empower each one differently?

Secondly: the good teacher has a vision for the class and a goal for each child. The vision might be that the class will be exposed to the Spanish culture this year. She'll play Spanish music, and teach the kids how to dance the Flamenco. A goal for half the class might be "speaking Spanish"; a goal for the other half might be "reading Spanish".

Does your boss have a vision for this coming year? Is this vision hung on the wall, and talked about often? And does he have a goal for you to reach? Does this goal fit you and fit the vision at the same time?

And thirdly: good teachers teach their children how to learn. Some kids learn by reading; some learn by listening. But if they're learning, they're asking questions. Good teachers are not interested in teaching reading, writing and 'rithmatic. They want to teach children how to learn. Learning comes from asking questions.

Does your boss give you the kind of assignments that cause you to ask all sorts of questions? And does he give you the authority and responsibility to figure out the answers? And does he hold you accountable for those answers?

Good leaders and good teachers do three things:

>They think about you constantly.

>They give you a vision and a goal.

>They teach you how to learn.

SHE MAKES ME ASK PERMISSION

"Dear Dr. C.,

"My boss won't let me do anything! I've been here for five years, and I know what I'm doing. But she makes me run to her for permission. I'm losing my self-confidence.

"This isn't helping me a bit. What should I do, Dr. C.?

Signed: "Jonathon"

Many of us - at work - ask permission, but how many ask forgiveness? The majority would say: the prudent thing is for us to ask permission.

That may be the prudent thing for the moment. If I'm about to do a risky thing, like sign a big contract, or agree to a big settlement - even though it's within my job parameters, it's probably prudent - for the moment - to ask permission.

However, for the long run, it may be the worst possible decision I can make.

I remember a young man who worked for me years ago. His name was Stan. Stan was intelligent, experienced, and extremely loyal. I could not have asked for anything more. Well, maybe one thing more. You see, Stan came to me for everything; he never made a decision. No matter what the issue, he had to have my permission. This went on for a year and a half. Then one day, I just had to fire him.

In the long run, it really is better to ask forgiveness than to continually ask permission.

What are we afraid of? We know our jobs. We probably know it better than our boss does. We know what would be a good risk, and what would be a bad one. Why ask permission from our boss? Just do it. If it turns out to be wrong, apologize. What's the big deal?

Sometimes, however, our companies make us do these silly things.

Have you ever tried to pay for your groceries with a personal check? A very capable cashier has to stop everything, page the manager, and wait for him to arrive. It takes him forever to get there, but when he finally makes it, he looks at your check, then at you (as if he could tell by your face that your check won't bounce) then he scribbles his initials and hands it to the cashier. What a waste of time and manpower!

Here's a good test for you. If you work at a place that has three shifts like a hospital or a police station, look at the decisions that are made by the night crew. They don't have the Administration around to ask. So they just do it.

If your boss has the self-confidence to make her own decisions, she must trust you – that you have the knowledge and the confidence to make your own decisions.

Self-confidence
Grows like a muscle –
With lots of exercise.

SHE HAS NO SELF-CONFIDENCE

"Dear Dr. C.,

"My boss is a lovely lady. She's hard working, intelligent and fair, but she's a pushover. People walk all over her. I want her to stand up and take charge, but she backs off and remains silent.

"Can a person like this ever change?"

Signed: *"Roger"*

This is an unusual email. Most of the questions I receive talk about bosses who are so full of self-confidence that it bubbles over into arrogance. Most employees complain that their boss is too tough, not too soft.

However, a boss who won't speak up or stand up for her employees can be just as frustrating as the bully. So this boss must change, too, if she's going to be successful.

Change is always difficult, but especially in this case. Here's a woman who no doubt has great talent and knowledge, and who understands her company and her job and all the daily issues connected with it. But when faced with a strong personality, someone who talks louder and bolder, she steps down.

Can she ever change? Can this reserved woman, this "lovely lady", ever hold up her hand and say: "Wait a minute! You're wrong about this"?

Of course, she can. But it's going to take a lot of practice. And she will need a mentor, somebody who will guide her through this jungle of new behavior.

This is what she must burn into her head, and repeat every day:

"I can never be absolutely positive that I'm right, but I will speak up anyway – because the other person is not absolutely sure of his position, either."

After each confrontation, she will meet with her mentor, and re-enact the scene. She will discover ways to be more forceful and still maintain her dignity. She will see that silence doesn't always bring serenity, and she will gradually learn which battles to fight, and which ones to leave for another day.

"Lovely ladies" can also be "legendary leaders". Remember:

The small saw that's sharp
Cuts more wood
Than the large saw that's dull.

SHE DOESN'T HAVE PRODUCT KNOWLEDGE

"Dear Dr. C.,

"We have a new boss. She has many years of experience in managing but she knows nothing about our business.

"We'll have to start educating her the minute she comes in the door, and she's never going to know as much as I do.

"How can I ever respect a boss like that?"

Signed: *"Terry".*

Terry is not alone in this feeling of frustration. I can't tell you how many times I've received emails just like this one. And, although Terry doesn't mention it here, I'm sure there's a little bit of jealousy and maybe even anger – because Terry didn't get the job.

But the question is valid. Do you hire an accountant to manage an engineering unit? Can a fireman become a police chief? Can a used car salesman become the mayor of a city?

Most of us would say "no". We would agree with Terry that industry experience is required for any leadership position. But most of us would be wrong.

To be a boss – to be a leader of any group or any unit or any organization – does not require industry knowledge. I don't have to know the zipper industry to be the president of YKK. I don't have to know the insurance business to be the owner and president of GEICO. I'll have to learn it in a hurry – that's for sure – just like Warren Buffet did. But it's not industry knowledge that makes a good leader.

In fact, many times, industry *ignorance* can help. I can hear Terry's new boss saying: "Terry, you know more about this than I do; give me your suggestion". With this statement, she has begun to build a strong, loyal team with the one man who resented her from the start.

Our best leaders can leap from industry to industry. They can move from making zippers to selling car insurance. Their products do not define great leaders; they are defined by their people-skills.

The question is not: can they sell the product? The question is:

*Can they
motivate
their people?*

YOU CAN'T DO THAT!

Dear Dr. C.,

Every year, our executives go away for a few days to do "Strategic Planning". I've often wondered what it was. They come back all "revved up", and ready to roll. How does it work?"

Signed: "Julius".

Last week I was in Birmingham, Alabama with a group of these executives. I was helping them work out their strategic plan for next year. But as I sat there listening to them, I thought:" why don't individuals do this?" Why don't we do an individual strategic plan?

Most of us just go from year to year, and take what we get. But companies get what they take. They take hold of their future; they make their future happen.

Wouldn't you like to have a crystal ball that would tell you what your future really could be?

Strategic planning comes with four questions. If you can answer these four questions, you can begin to lay the foundations for the kind of life you'll be living next year.

Over the past several years, I have helped 72 companies do this. Most of them take 2 days to grapple with these 4 questions, some take a week. But you could do it in less than an hour. In less than 60 minutes, you could begin to take hold of your future.

This is the crystal ball called strategic planning. These are the four questions every organization asks itself each year. And these are the same questions you can ask yourself- if you want to take control of your future:

First: What are my strengths? Organizations look at their products and services; but you should look at your talents and interests. What do you like doing? What is it that makes you bounce out of bed in the morning when you know you're going to do "this" today? Write all your strengths down on paper.

Second: What are my weaknesses? Each one of us has a set of weaknesses. If I'm good at talking, I'm weak at listening. If I'm good at detail work; I'm weak at finishing on time. But if you have trouble finding your weaknesses, just ask the person you live with. And then write those down on the same paper.

Third: What are my opportunities? This is where you decide what you want. If you want a higher paying job, and you're a good student, you might decide to go back to school. If you're good at painting and drawing and crafts, you could open up your own shop. Write down what you want to do.

Fourth: What are the threats? What are the forces that will try to destroy my opportunities? Some will come from outside, like money and contacts, but most will come from inside you. You will hear that familiar voice that whispers; "you can't do that".

But if you're going to be a strategic planner, you will say: "this is my opportunity. I've got the strengths, and I can overcome or delegate my weaknesses, and I will not allow any threats to stop me – especially myself. The future is mine to make.

I will not take what I get;
I will get what I take."

Behind Your Back

BUILD LASTING RELATIONSHIPS

Bill Cummings (Dr. C)

HE DOESN'T KNOW THE GAME

"Dear Dr. C.

"The little league baseball season has begun, and my two sons are playing. One belongs to the Braves and the other to the Pirates. Today we've got to beat the Yankees and the Orioles. And I think this kind of competition is great.

"But when I come to work the next morning, I find my boss fostering the same kind of competition between two of our departments. And I have to wonder: is this really healthy?"

Signed: "Jerry"

I've wondered the same thing for years. Why do we compete with each other in the same company?

I can understand Ford competing with Chevrolet, or Sears competing with Belks, or McDonald's competing with Burger King, but why would one region compete with another region in the same company?

But many organizations do this, don't they?

I have known some presidents who actually promoted this kind of internal fighting. One of them called it "the survival of the compulsive overachievers". He based his philosophy on a book written by the president of Revlon back in 1976. The idea was simple: the manager of the winning division will be promoted, and the manager of the losing division will be fired. It sounds a bit like Jack Welsh of recent GE fame who fired 10% of his workforce every year.

I don't buy it.

I think every company and every division and every manager and every worker should compete against their own records of last year or last month. Just like a golfer. But that's where the competition stops.

The other division or the other department is another member of my team. I don't compete with them; I cooperate with them -the way all the kids on the baseball team cooperate with each other. Those kids know who's on their team, and who isn't. And they support each other. They know that they all win or they all lose together; the catcher can't win while the pitcher is losing.

Members of Congress miss the point, also. They should be cooperating with each other to make the United States better able to compete in the global market. Instead, they're competing against each other for local pork.

I think it's time for all of us to look closely again at our children's little league teams. Check out those uniforms. And then ask ourselves:

Who's on our team?
And
Who really is our competition?

Bill Cummings (Dr. C)

HE'S A "GOOD OLE BOY"

"Dear Dr. C.,

"I joined this company recently with 20 years of experience. Last week, my boss hires this friend of his – who has no experience – and gives him a higher position and a higher salary. This is pure "good ole boy favoritism", and I'm sick of it. What can I do?"

Signed: *"Debbie."*

Let's ask the question: Why do bosses do this? If you can do the job, and you're already in the company, why would a boss go outside?

Is it, as Debbie put it, "good ole boy favoritism", and nothing else?

It could be. I think we've all seen that in the past. Both men and women bosses trying to fill their departments with relatives and friends who have no skills and no talents and no experience.

But I don't see that very much any more. What I'm seeing around the country is this: a manager has an obligation to hit a target. He's got to get his numbers, and he needs to surround himself with people he can trust. He naturally looks to people he worked with before. People in the company he came from. They're not necessarily his friends, but he knows their work ethic. He can trust them to deliver the numbers. In fact, some companies reward their associates with a bonus if they recommend somebody who eventually gets hired.

It's not so much the "good ole boy system" as it is the "good ole family system". As companies grow bigger, they're trying to maintain the culture they had when they were smaller. The culture where everybody knows everybody else, and can trust him or her completely.

I know this hurts – when you're not a part of their family. You want to be trusted and respected too. But that takes time- not past experience in another family. You need past experience in this family.

In many cases,
It's really not favoritism;
It's survival.

Bill Cummings (Dr. C)

SHE HAS IT "HER WAY"

"Dear Dr. C.,

"You remember Frank Sinata's famous song: "My Way". It's my boss's theme song. She thinks she's delegating to us, but if we don't do it her way, it just won't fly. It's her way, or no way.

Signed: "Ann."

Employees like Ann have a special kind of suffering. They know their job. They know the end result. And they know how to get that result –their way. But if they don't do it—their boss's way --it's a failure.

It's just like grade school, isn't it? Our children are told that there is only one way to learn history or geography or science. They must read it. And if they can't read – if they can't do it "the reading way", they can't be promoted to the next grade.

But reading isn't the only way to learn. A child can learn history by listening, by watching films, by traveling to the sites. To punish a child with dyslexia, for example, because he cannot read; to keep this child from advancing with his classmates – because he cannot learn the way his teacher learned – is just as criminal as the boss who demands "her way" at work.

We're not asking the right questions at work or at school. At work, the question should be: "what's the end result?" If an employee can complete the project on time, within budget and according to the specifications – who cares how he did it? If a boss is asking the question: "Did you do it my way?" it's simply the wrong question.

At school, the question should be: what's the information the child should know?" If the child can learn the information from the computer with spell check, a calculator or a movie – who cares? "Reading a book" is not the only way. And it's not any way at all for a dyslexic child.

Frank Sinata's song: "My Way" should apply not to bosses and teachers but to workers and students. Every worker and every student must be allowed to do it their way.

*"Every child can learn
and every worker can perform.
But each one will do it
differently.*

Bill Cummings (Dr. C)

HE SHOUTS

"Dear Dr. C.,

"My boss is passionate about our business. He's excited when we make our goals, and he's upset when we miss them. He shouts when we succeed and he shouts when we fail. This intimidates a lot of employees, but I think it's great. What do you think, Dr. C?"

Signed, "Martha".

I think it's not what he does, but how he does it. It's not what he says; it's how he says it.

I went to my grandson's little league baseball game the other night. Austin is 7 years old. As you can imagine, boys his age need a lot of support from their fathers. There were dads all over the field, shouting encouragement and direction, and screaming as these little kids hit the ball and ran around the bases.

However, I also heard the dads screaming at a bad call, and moaning when errors were made. But I never heard any of them scream or moan at the kids. I never heard any of them embarrass or intimidate any of the boys —on either team. They hollered and screamed and moaned; they were passionate about the game. But they were compassionate about the players.

It wasn't what they said; it was the way they said it.

I think the same can be said about the work place. The game of business should be very exciting; we have every right to be passionate about the work we're doing. There's nothing wrong with shouting and screaming and ringing the bell – when we make a great sale. And there's nothing wrong with moaning and groaning when we lose out to our competitor.

A boss can feel very passionate about the company's revenue and he can say to you:" our profits are down; what happened?" But the way in which he asks that question – not the words that he uses –will determine whether you feel challenged and motivated to find the answer, or whether you feel intimidated and motivated to run and hide.

It's not whether you shout and scream and moan,
it's how you do it
that counts.

Bill Cummings (Dr. C)

RELATIONSHIPS NEED SECURITY

"Dear Dr.C.,

"My boss is so insecure, she can't trust us to build a lasting relationship. She's paranoid. She thinks we're talking about her in the break room when she walks in.

"How can we build a lasting team with that kind of an attitude?

Signed: "Virginia".

You've heard the phrase: "familiarity breeds contempt". That means we show respect immediately to strangers, but once we get to know a person, respect is slower to come.

Why is that?

You've seen nurses walk into a patient's room and shower this stranger with care and concern and deep respect, and then huff and puff back to the nurses station where she barely speaks to people she's known for 10 years.

Why is that?

It's the same thing in our homes, isn't it? When the neighbors come over for dinner, they get the best china and silverware, but the next day, our own family gets plastic.

Why is that?

Take a look around your work place. Who are the people who are showing respect to everyone, and who are the people who show respect only to strangers? You know what I mean. Some of our fellow workers treat us like teenagers in a high school lunchroom. They treat a corporate visitor like he was Troy Aikman come back to play football, but they won't even share a coke with us.

Why is that?

I think I know why. And it's painfully simple. There are two kinds of people who come to work every day. The secure. And the insecure. The secure woman feels good about herself, and sincerely wants to help other people. The insecure woman feels lousy about herself, and constantly wants strangers (who don't know the truth about her) to like her. She thinks that people who already know her can't really like what they see.

Respect starts with me. I have to respect myself. I have to give myself the best china from time to time. Every day as I drive into work, I need to say:

"I have a lot of faults, and I make a lot of mistakes, and sometimes I'm moody and sometimes I'm angry and sometimes I talk too much. But I'm okay. And you know what? So is everybody else who works with me".

And all this needs to start with your boss.

Familiarity breeds contempt –
only
when I'm unfamiliar with my true self.

Bill Cummings (Dr. C)

HE LABELS EVERYONE

"Dear Dr.C.,

"My boss has a clever name for everyone. 'Slow Suzie', 'Hard-hearted Hannah', 'Blustery Bill'., etc.

"Sometimes it's funny; but most of the time, it hits hard and low, and we resent it.

Signed: "Anonymous"

Have you ever noticed how we stereotype people at work? We call this person "slow" and this one "fast". We label this extrovert "arrogant" and this introvert "lazy". And this sticks like glue. It never changes. It doesn't matter what the person does.

That "arrogant person" can act humble and kind and generous – it doesn't matter. In our minds, she will always be arrogant. And we will always think of her that way.

Teachers see this happening in their classrooms every day. The "in-crowd" labels the "nerds"; the jocks label the kids to be avoided. High school and college fraternities and sororities segregate people very quickly.

In our businesses and organizations, we have the blacks and the whites, the executives and the workers, the Republicans and the Democrats, the men and the women. And there's a set stereotype for each one. Nobody gets a chance to break out of that mold.

I know some very intelligent people in our community who truly believe that every Republican is a greedy, selfish, heartless imperialist who wants to jail the homeless. And others who believe that every Democrat is a Robin Hood who wants to steal from the rich and give it all to the poor.

The word "stereotype" is a relatively new word for this ancient practice. It comes from an 1817 French printing press. It was the

French word for their wrought-iron cast. But it's the word we use for a problem that has existed since the beginning of time.

For us, this word identifies the wrought-iron casts in our minds that print out oversimplified opinions, prejudiced attitudes, and uncritical judgments which all of us live by every day of our lives.

How do you break a wrought-iron cast? With a sledgehammer.

It takes a deliberate and consistent pounding to break through years and years of stereotypical prejudice. What was built up over generations of traditions will not be wiped out in one moment.

Governor Sonny Purdue and former President Jimmy Carter teamed up in '04 to swing the sledgehammer at our black-white stereotypes. They formed a task force to DO something about it. This needs to be continued at every level, in every school, in every church, in every business in our state.

But that's just one. We have so many stereotypes.

If you want to start breaking down your own stereotypes, try this: think of the person at work you really don't like, and do something nice for that person today.

A random act of kindness.
Is the best sledgehammer
We have.

Bill Cummings (Dr. C)

WHERE SHOULD I MOVE?

"Dear Dr. C.,

"I'm young and single, and I've lived all my life in Central Georgia. I know you have lived all over the world. If you were I, what town or what country would attract you? Where would you go to make your fortune?"

Signed: "Jennifer".

How many of you have asked this question?

I spent the last two weeks traveling with my family through Montana, Idaho and Utah. We met people from all over the world. A Japanese family sat next to us in Yellowstone Park as we watched Old Faithful explode 200 feet in the air. In a small town in Idaho we met a retired man from California, and in Park City, Utah, we stayed with people from Norway.

Very few people pick the spot where they want to live; most just go where the job takes them. But what if you could choose? What if you could pick exactly where you would live the rest of your life? Where would that be?

I've heard many people talk about moving to Atlanta, but when I worked in Atlanta, I heard many of those people say they'd prefer to get of the rat race and move to Gray or Forsyth.

The retired man I met in Idaho last week said he hated California and was glad he moved to a small country town in Idaho, but a few minutes later he was telling me how backwards this Idaho town really is.

So where should you live? Where should you go to make your fortune? In my experience, it doesn't matter. You can live anywhere in the world. You can live in the Utah mountains or the California sunshine, or you can live right here in Central Georgia.

The key, of course, is one thing: "do you like yourself"? Do you get up every morning and look in the mirror before you go to work, and say: in spite of all my flaws, and all my failings, I do like that person in the mirror."?

If you can do that, you can live anywhere. And the reason is obvious. No matter where we move, we take ourselves along.

Geography
Does not change
Integrity

Bill Cummings (Dr. C)

HE HAS NO TACT

"Dear Dr. C.,

"When it comes to tactful, my boss is clueless. He chews us out in public. He doesn't care if we're embarrassed. He moves fast and furious, and expects us to do the same.

"When we complain, he has three favorite phrases: One: 'get over it'. Two: business is not a baby shower' and Three: 'if you can't stand the heat, get out of the kitchen.'

"What do you think, Dr. C.? Am I just too sensitive?

Signed: *"Hazel".*

There are two answers here, I think. The first is: 'no boss has the right to be tactless'. Truthful, yes, tactless, no. But the second answer is: 'sensitive employees really must 'get over it'.

Let's examine both.

A tactless boss is a hard driving, no nonsense type of person who simply wants to get the job done. He or she (because women can be tactless, too) feels that honesty is not only the best policy, but the quickest, too. And speed is of the essence.

These people are not embarrassed or hurt by their tactless bosses, so they really don't understand why you should feel any different. In fact, they think that you're weak and insecure if you can't take the brunt of their attacks.

Every tactless boss needs a wake-up call; a whack on the side of the head; a loud whistle in their ear. "Hello. People are different. Just because some people are more sensitive than you, that does not make them less productive."

However, sensitive employees need a little "shaking up" also. The business world really isn't 'home sweet home'. We try to make our work place as pleasant as possible, (and we should) but our boss is not our mommy. Our boss is held responsible for our productivity. When a department fails to reach the quota, the supervisor fails. Sensitive employees need to give the boss some slack.

The work place is a "make-believe" environment. It is not natural. People are placed in positions of leading and following based on seniority and education, not on nature.

If your organization is dysfunctional, it might be because your bosses are too tactless and your employees are too sensitive.

It takes work
To make
Work
Work.

Bill Cummings (Dr. C)

HE CAN'T BUILD RELATIONSHIPS

"Dear Dr. C.,

"My boss is a wonderful, talented doctor who has absolutely no bedside manners. He knows everything about medicine but nothing about relationships. He can cure diseases but he can't carry on a conversation.

"Don't they teach this in medical school"?

Signed: "a dedicated nurse."

When I received this email, I called Dr. Rob Hash, the assistant dean at Mercer's medical school and found out that each student at that school takes a two-year course called <u>Clinical Skills.</u> Dr. Hash will let me audit this class next month when it starts up again. But he told me that he couldn't speak for the other 159 medical schools. Each one has a different curriculum.

But doctors aren't the only ones who find it difficult to build relationships at work. How many bosses do you know who look like doctors on the way to surgery?

They're in suits instead of scrubs; they're waving schedules instead of scalpels; but they always seem to have the same life and death deadline.

They have no time for chitchat. They'll talk to you about your reports; they'll listen as you describe an irate customer; they'll prescribe solutions to your problems. But that's it! You never hear: "how was your vacation?" Or "how's your sick child?" Or "where would you like to go in this company?"

Building relationships means spending time. For a doctor, that means every so often, going into the staff lounge after surgery instead of the doctors' lounge, and just listening to the nurses.

For a boss in an office, it means walking around every day, learning the names of the spouse and the children, and what's important to them.

But many bosses feel this is a waste of time. They feel they're here to perform a task, not to build a relationship. All they need to know about an employee is whether or not he can do the job.

But they forget that all of us work better and smarter and more efficient, when:

Our boss thinks enough of us
To spend time
With us.

Bill Cummings (Dr. C)

YESTERDAY AND TODAY

"Dear Dr. C.,

"Are bosses really better now than they used to be?

"Nearly all of my bosses are 30 or 40 years old. When we complain about their policies, they tell us how lucky we are. They tell us horror stories about the white, male, sexist, chauvinistic pigs they had as bosses.

Tell me, dr. C.; were bosses really that bad in the 60's and 70's? You were there."

Signed: Mary.

Yes, I was there. In fact, I was one of those bosses. In 1975, I had a corner office in the tallest building in downtown Macon. There were 10 of us then- all vice presidents, and we were running the fastest growing business in Georgia. Within 5 years, our stock had gone from $1.00 a share to $50.00 a share and had split 7 times. We had over 8000 employees.

Were we bad bosses? Well, we were all white males, and we were certainly chauvinistic, and we didn't know much about empowerment and involvement. But were we better than the bosses who trained us?

I remember my first boss. It was the summer of 1946, and Mr. Whipple owned the corner grocery store on the south side of Chicago. He hired me to deliver groceries on my bicycle.

He'd put the grocery bag in my wire basket, give me the address, look at his watch, and tell me to get moving. When I returned, he'd look at his watch again, and say: "okay, where did you go after the delivery?" He didn't trust me the whole summer.

Have bosses become more trusting, more open, and more participative than they were in 1946? Absolutely. Are they more inclusive and less sexist and racist than they were in 1975? Of course. But could our bosses today get any better? You bet, they could.

I've been watching bosses grow for nearly 60 years. One generation after another. Each one looks at the strengths and weaknesses of those who went before, and then they make their own choices.

The truly great bosses I have known – in every generation - are those who sit down behind their wooden desks in their large corner offices, and they say:

I have not
Arrived.
I am just
Becoming.

Bill Cummings (Dr. C)

LEADERSHIP 101

"Dear Dr. C.,

"I'm a brand new manager. Monday morning will be my first day at leading a group of people. I think I'm qualified – at least, the company thinks so – but I don't know if my 9 employees think so.

"I'm a little scared and a little nervous. Can you give me anything to hang on to?

Signed: "Janice"

I wish Janice could have been with me yesterday morning. I had breakfast at Maebob's in Irwinton, GA. The owner of the restaurant came in and he sat at my table. They call him "Pops".

My favorite waitress, Nora, came over with his breakfast, and I asked her this question:

"Nora, you've been working for Pops for 8 years. What does he do that you like?"

Both of them laughed, and then Nora said three things that I wish Janice and all the managers in the world could hear.

She said: "Well, I know what my job is, and he lets me do it".

"Okay", I said, "What else?"

"I'm only human" she added, "and I make mistakes, and he tells me when I do something wrong"

"And you like that?" I asked.

"Sure" she said. "How else can I improve?"

"Okay", I said, "Anything else?"

"Yes. He makes me feel good when I do the right things."

That's it. It's not rocket science. Nora very quickly identified all three elements of leadership.

Number one: _Empowerment._ From the very beginning, Pops laid out his goal for Maebob's, which must be something like: "Treat every customer like family". Nora knows how to do that, and Pops does not micromanage her.

Number two: _Coaching._ When Nora makes a mistake, Pops is right there to help her correct it.

And number three: _Recognition and Reward_. When Nora has customers raving about her and the restaurant, Pops praises her and thanks her.

Thousands of books have been written about this, and hundreds of thousands of seminars have been given.

But if you want to see this in action, just drive up to Irwinton, GA., and have breakfast at Maebob's.

*I call it
Leadership 101*

Bill Cummings (Dr. C)

MAKING MISTAKES

Dear Dr. C.,

"My boss treats me like I make mistakes on purpose. He must think I drive to work dreaming up new ways to screw up. Sure, I make mistakes. Doesn't everyone?"

Signed: *"Frank"*

If I have learned anything from my consulting business, I have learned this: you want to do a good job today. You have every intention of doing the right thing. Your job is important to you; either you really love the work, or you need the paycheck. Either way, making deliberate mistakes is never an option.

But we do make mistakes, don't we? All of us.

We don't intend to; we don't want to; we don't plan these mistakes. But we do make them. And sometimes, these mistakes cost us our job. But did you know that in many cases, this does not have to be the end result?

Over the years, I have worked with organizations around the world. And I have seen some of the biggest errors you could imagine. And I have learned four secrets that you can learn that will determine whether your mistakes will bring you failure, or bring you growth.

A teller in a bank is trained to count money. What does she do when she comes up short? A truck driver is trained to drive safely. What does he do when he's caught speeding? What kinds of things do you do?

Here are four things I suggest:

> One: admit it.
> Two: apologize
> Three: find the root cause.
> Four: accept the consequences.

Number one: Admit it. I suppose the lawyers are screaming: "No-never admit it." But I'm saying – if you did it, say so: "it looks like I screwed up". Just be open and honest.

Some of our political leaders have given us just the opposite example. To hear their TV ad's, you'd think they never made a mistake in their entire lives.

Number two: Apologize. You remember the movie: "Love Story"? The actress says; "Love means never having to say you're sorry". Don't believe it. I've been in love with the same woman for 40 years, and I can't tell you how many times I've said, "I'm sorry".

Number three: Find the root cause. Why would a trained teller come up short? She can admit it, and even apologize to her boss, but if she doesn't focus on why she did it, she will no doubt do it again. Did she do her counting while listening to a lot of chatter all around her? Did she stay up late the night before? What's the root cause of her mistake?

Number four: Accept the consequences. What if two bank tellers, Julie and Mary, made exactly the same mistake in exactly the same way, for exactly the same reason. However, Julie's mistake cost the bank $200; whereas Mary's cost $150,000. Both women admitted it; both apologized and both identified the same root cause. But does Mary get fired? Probably. The punishment doesn't fit the crime. The punishment fits the consequences. Don't scream: "Life is not fair". Just accept the consequences, and get on with your life.

When you make a mistake, admit it, apologize, find the root cause, and accept the consequences.

*Anything else –
Just makes you a bad politician.*

Bill Cummings (Dr. C)

THE BIG BALANCE

"Dear Dr. C.,

"I can't seem to please my boss. She always wants more. She pushes us to hit unreasonable targets, and then, when we actually hit them, (by some miracle)- she yells and screams for more.

"I want my job to be challenging and exciting, but this is ridiculous. Both my health and my home-life are suffering.

"What can I do, Dr. C.?"

Signed: Don.

How many of you feel this way? As you get ready to go to work in the morning, do you have a tight knot in your belly, and a slight nausea?

Are you under deadlines like the news media? Are you held accountable for 100% accuracy like surgeons and anesthesiologists? Do you face life and death situations like the police and firemen?

Or is your day boring? Are you wondering why you should even get out of bed? Do you have the kind of job that will get done whether you go or not? The kind of boss who doesn't even know your name? The kind of responsibilities that anybody else can do?

Most of us try to avoid the two extremes, don't we? We don't want to be bored silly, but we don't want to be driven to drink, either. We want jobs that make us want to get up in the morning, but jobs that we can leave when we come back home.

Is this asking too much? Is this utopia?

No. It is not asking too much. This is the job of management. This is what each boss must do. A boss in a "high-stress industry" like the media or the operating room must bring calm and patience and serenity. The work itself will provide the challenge and the excitement.

A boss in a "low-stress industry" like a manufacturing plant or a large corporate office must generate the excitement every day–through games and competition and rallies.

Every job must be balanced. However:

Behind every balanced
job
Is a balanced
boss.

CONCLUSION

Most of the bosses I know are balanced. They are sincere, dedicated, hard-working men and women who want the best for their people, their parishioners, their clients, or their children.

You may be one of them. You may be a manager, a pastor, a lawyer, or a parent.

Your perception is:

> "I'm a good coach.
> "I make good decisions.
> "I listen intently to my people.
> "I communicate clearly and on a timely basis.
> "I'm a person of integrity who "walks the talk".
> "My self-confidence is not arrogance.
> "I build lasting relationships"

What is their perception? What is the perception of the people who depend on you? Is it the same? When it comes to leadership,

"Perception is Reality."

I may think I'm good at listening, and poor in communication, but my people may think just the opposite. I may be convinced that I show strong self-confidence, but my people may perceive it as intimidating.

Would you like to find out?

If you're a manager or pastor or professional, give the following test to your people. Have them fill it out ANONYMOUSLY, and give their answers to a 3rd party (outside consultant, HR, or some other person) who will collate the responses and give you the summary. You'll be glad you did.

PLEASE GIVE ME FEEDBACK

YOUR ANSWERS WILL BE COLLATED ANONYMOUSLY

PLEASE BE AS CANDID AS YOU CAN.

This is True:

Seldom	Sometimes	Often	Nearly Always
1	2	3	4

1. Overall, my management style is "coaching", not bossing. I don't intimidate or embarrass or "dictate" ____

2. I make good decisions – after I have heard your opinions and suggestions ____

3. When I listen to you, I am totally present, and show you great respect even when I disagree ____

4. I am a good communicator. I neither exaggerate nor hoard information, and I give it to you on a timely basis ____

5. I don't make promises I can't keep. If I say I'm going to do it, I do it. And when I do it, it's fair for everyone ____

6. I am self-confident, but I am not arrogant. I do not intimidate or embarrass people in public. ____

7. I am in this for the long run. I build long-lasting relationships based on compassion and understanding and fairness. ____

Bill Cummings (Dr. C)

Where you scored me a 1 or 2 – please write in the behavior you feel I should improve.

And thank you very much for this. I will do this again in 6 months to see if I have improved in these areas.

QUOTES FROM EXECUTIVES

"Bill Cummings has such a marvelous ability to arrive immediately at the core of a problem, and deliver wisdom in small, succinct and understandable doses."
    Juanita Jordan, President
    Peyton Anderson Foundation.

"Dr. C. showed me that it isn't enough to have an open door policy; sometimes you have to walk out of that door, go down the hall, and be proactive in soliciting the opinions and concerns of the folks who work for you".
    Chap McMichael, Vice-President
    Electro-Mech Scoreboard Co.

"Bill Cummings has been an invaluable help to our Company for years. 'Behind Your Back' is a wonderful collection of lessons that are right on target. The only thing better is to receive these lessons from him in person".
    Bob Hatcher, President,
    MidCountry Financial Corporation

"Dr. C. elevates the art of listening to the nth degree. He teaches us through example to "hear" what people actually say, not what we want or think they are saying. This is a 'must read' for every new or seasoned boss"
    Ethel Cullinan, President
    Medcen Community Health Foundation

"American business is exceptional at developing managers, and generally a failure at producing leaders. Now along comes this little book that demonstrates for managers an easy-to-follow roadmap to leadership".
    Ray Enderle, Retired Director,
    Sunoco, Inc.

Bill Cummings (Dr. C)

"Dr.C. states excellent management techniques in the form of responses to questions from employees. He has provided the help all of us managers need in identifying problem behaviors and finding solutions".
Mike Ford, President
NewTown Macon, Inc.

"Managers need to accept the fact that 'perception is never wrong', just sometimes different from what was intended. If they're willing to listen and change, they'll be glad they asked for the feedback."
Don Karell, VP and GM, Alabama
Charter Communications, Inc.

"Bill Cummings has hit a home run. So many times we know what to do but we're just too busy to take the time to do it right. Managers should carry this book in their back pocket; part of their 'uniform of the day'".
Bill Wiley, Retired Vice President,
YKK-USA

"A fun read... informative, practical, direct... you'll find yourself saying: 'When was Dr. C. in our office? Sounds like he's talking about us'. Dr. C. is a consultant par excellence!"
Dr. Betty Scott, President,
International Leadership Institute.

"Practical, down-to-earth, accessible and helpful to all audiences"
Dr. Kirby Godsey, President,
Mercer University

Printed in the United States
109742LV00002B/853-948/A